From This Day Forward

Blueprint for Family Happiness

D0034300

From This Day Forward
Blueprint for Family Happiness

Nancy Van Pelt

author of
The Compleat Parent
The Compleat Marriage
The Compleat Tween
The Compleat Courtship
How to Communicate With Your Mate
How to Develop Your Child's Character
For information on these books, contact the publisher.

REVIEW AND HERALD PUBLISHING ASSOCIATION
Washington, DC 20039-0555
Hagerstown, MD 21740

This book was
Edited by Richard W. Coffen
Designed by Richard Steadham
Cover art by Richard Steadham
Type set: 10/11 Times Roman

PRINTED IN U.S.A.

Library of Congress Cataloging in Publication Data

Van Pelt, Nancy L.
    From this day forward.

    1. Family—United States. 2. Domestic relations—
United States. 3. Parent and child—United States.
4. Courtship—United States. I. Title.
HQ536.V36   1985   306.8'5'0973   85-8244
ISBN 0-8280-0280-0

Contents

Chapter 1

The Family

—Laying a Solid Foundation for a Solid Future

The thing most lacking in the American home today is the family. (But remember that American still ends with "I can!")

On January 25, 1971, multitudes of joyful Ugandans thronged the streets of Kampala. A popular soldier had just dethroned their detested leader, Milton Obote. "This is the year of peace, love, unity, and reconciliation," the new ruler asserted. "I have no bad intentions from now onward. I want to be very friendly to the entire world."

The popular soldier? Idi Amin.

Because of his six-foot-four-inch, three-hundred-pound frame, Amin came to be known affectionately as "Big Daddy." But soon strange rumors began making the rounds. Could Idi Amin really be the gruesome savage that gossip made him out to be? Yes. The accusations were all too true, and by the end of his eight-year reign, Big Daddy had butchered at least 300,000 of his own people.

Whispered tales of unimaginable sadism, stories of atrocities inside the pink stucco building that housed the State Research Bureau, accounts of Saturday orgies of forced sex and brutality under Big Daddy's twinkling eyes, recitals of pregnant women being disemboweled by Amin's soldiers, fueled the nightmares that tortured the psyches of Ugandans everywhere.

Amid this holocaust lived Kosea Kalebu, his wife, and twelve children—a close, warm, and loving family. The large Kalebu house was situated on ten acres near the Ugandan capital of Kampala. Kosea had built the spacious home large enough to accommodate the entire Kalebu family as well as relatives and friends whom the children asked to visit.

Kosea Kalebu was not only an outstanding professor of engineering at the University of Kampala but also a devout Christian. Amin, however, had vowed to kill anyone who was not Moslem. So his soldiers shut down churches, and all Christian activities were forced underground. Despite this taboo, Kosea Kalebu worked tirelessly and diligently for his church. Though no one worshiped there any longer, the churches still had to be cared for—inside and out. And in addition to the physical upkeep of the churches, much spiritual work still needed to be carried out by the mission and the pastors. With no churches in which couples could be married, the Kalebu house, because of its spaciousness, was the place many couples chose for their wedding ceremonies. Beautiful baskets of cut flowers would adorn the home. The furniture would be rearranged. And glowing brides and solemn grooms would repeat their wedding vows in the quiet charm of the Kalebu home.

For eight long and troubled years Kosea Kalebu served his God, his family, and society, during which time three attempts were made on his life. His life was in constant peril. Early in April, 1979, conditions in Uganda got even worse. And one Thursday evening the Kalebu family spent half the night in prayer. The next morning Kosea announced, "I'm not going to the university today. I can't teach anymore. Everything is in chaos. The students aren't free to come to classes. Amin's soldiers, armed with machine guns, have set up roadblocks everywhere. I'm going to stay home and work in my garden."

Later that morning Kosea called the family together for another prayer session. They had just finished praying when they heard shots outside their house. Amin's soldiers then kicked in the back door and stomped through the house. They wanted Kosea Kalebu.

It seemed as though these men were familiar with every inch of that large house, for they knew right where to go. Once they found Kosea, they demanded that he give them the money he had just received from the mission to give to the pastors whom he would secretly meet. Kosea refused. The soldiers opened fire, hitting him in the shoulder. As he collapsed into the arms of one of his sons the enraged soldiers grabbed the keys to the family car and spun out of the yard. Now bleeding badly, Kosea began to pray: "Dear God, please take care of my family, and whatever is Your will, let it be done."

Mother and children eased Father into a brother's car and began the ten-mile trip to the nearest medical facility. Under normal conditions they could have arrived there in minutes, but on this Friday they encountered roadblock after roadblock. At each one they had to explain their plight and go through the exasperating task of identifying themselves and showing their papers.

When they finally reached the hospital, Kosea was very weak. As kind attendants wheeled him into the operating room, the family prayed. But Kosea Kalebu—man of faith and greatly beloved by family and friends—died on the operating table, just two weeks before Amin was dethroned.

I had the privilege of meeting Rachel Kalebu, daughter of Kosea. She was obtaining an education in the United States at the time of her father's murder. Since she could not attend her father's funeral, she felt compelled to return for a visit, which she did in July of 1983. "The scene at the airport was the most difficult," Rachel related. "All my relatives were there to greet me—all but Father. At our family home I could almost hear his car coming up our driveway, and hear his voice calling me. He always called me 'Queen Judith.' It took me awhile to get used to Father's absence. We all loved him so much! His students called him 'the old man.' It's a term used with much respect there.''

Kosea Kalebu's story portrays but one of the thousands of tragedies that broke hearts in Uganda during Amin's reign of terror. Multitudes were wrenched from their families and brutally murdered. Now that Amin's rule is over, surviving family members continue to search for one another. You see, during the atrocities that Amin and his cohorts perpetrated, *no consideration* was given to preserving the family or continuing family lines.

Westerners find it difficult to fathom such tactics. Yet it seems to me that Americans are doing the same thing—only under a more ''civilized'' guise. Our families are being splintered and divided—not by force, as was the case in Uganda, but worse yet by *choice!* Shattered marriages, broken dreams, disintegrating relationships, emotionally confused children, have become the accepted norm of the twentieth century. Family members enjoy little continuity from one generation to the next. And this senseless destruction of priceless family ties occurs more and more frequently. Statistical studies indicate that half of American marriages now end in divorce. Too many of us live out life on the cafeteria plan—self-service only. We do what comes ''naturally,'' fight for our rights irrespective of the rights of others, put ourselves first, assert ourselves, and get even whenever we can.

Disillusioned men and women cast each other aside because their dreamed-of perfection always seems just beyond their grasp. Too many of us waste our lives searching for a perfect relationship that exists only in the caverns of our imaginations! A family may be under construction, but when it doesn't go according to the blueprint the partners leave it unfinished and begin searching for a more luxurious model. But they forget that the new family will be invaded by memories of the past, haunted by shadows of what has gone before. Nothing is big enough to blot out the memories of former places, people, holidays, and experiences.

When we keep on changing partners and breaking family ties, we destroy the continuity of family lineage. Security within the bonds of one family dissolves forever. And when gazing at photographs in the family album, we feel a hollowness of not "belonging." Whether breakup and remarriage was morally, ethically, or Biblically sound is hardly the issue when we embark on the fruitless search for a sense of personal family belonging among the ruins of a shattered home.

Too many Americans philosophize, "I'll stay with the family as long as I'm happy." But who of us has never experienced unhappiness? Haven't all of us from time to time felt like running away when the going got rough? It is imperative that the stability and continuance of the family run so deep through our subconscious that we cannot be touched by popular philosophy. When trouble hits our homes we must vow to work through the problem rather than run away from it. The continuance of family ties must come to mean more than splitting the family because of personal unhappiness or some inconvenience that we are temporarily enduring. Regardless of all the trials, outbursts, sharp words, injustices, unmet needs, and frustrated feelings, we all must come to recognize that the family is a *career,* a lifelong project. If we don't, before too long the family will become as endangered as the California condor!

Have you ever wondered, "What on earth can I do about this? I'm just one person in a fast-moving, impersonal world"? Well, let me tell you: You are not so insignificant as to have no influence. You *can* make a unique and important contribution within your circle of friends, because when *your* family is happy it will have a direct bearing on the families of friends as well as on the eventual happiness your own children will experience in marriage. Someone has estimated that every family directly influences twelve other families a year. If this ratio could be channeled into a positive avenue, the world could be changed!

The challenge for you today, then, is to follow the blueprint for family happiness so that others will see in your family God's power at work. Friends and neighbors will begin asking questions about the secrets of your successful family living, and your response will not fall on deaf ears. Right? Of course! When you see something that works in the lives of others, it causes you to stop, take notice, and question. For instance, if you see a family that has attained a successful, happy working relationship, you want to know how they have done it. If they have been saved from the brink of divorce, you ask, "How did they do it?" If some changes have taken place in their family, you wonder what caused the change.

Yes, the changes that occur in *you* can have a profound effect on others. Yet home can be the most difficult place on earth to practice something new! It is there—where things may seem the most hopeless, where others seem to work against you, and where you are the most tired and face the most trials—that *you* must begin to improve things. Every family member, of course, plays a vital role in the interplay of a successful family. But since I have access to no one but you, we'll talk about what *you* can do to enrich your home situation. *You* have a tremendous power to make your home approximate more closely God's idea of what a family should be. So my focus will be on *you*—how *you* can be a better person, a better companion, a better parent, a better communicator.

I have discovered that if left to their own instincts, families will take the route of least resistance. Left to their own inclinations, husbands and wives will join ranks with the one out of every two families that ends up in a divorce court instead of working through their problems. I have also discovered that in order to live successfully as a family we must check with the Master Architect of the family, who has left in His Word a blueprint for family living.

You need spend no more time on wishful thinking for a superior family life. The Bible offers clear advice about how to live successfully. God has provided you the needed blueprint so you can achieve exactly what your inner soul may be longing for—a happier lifestyle than you presently have.

This may seem a bit idealistic to you. You may be countering, "But you don't know what I've got to deal with at home!" I may not be aware of your specific circumstances, but one thing I can tell you: I have dealt with similar problems in other families. Hundreds, maybe thousands, of individual, perplexing, heartbreaking problems can surface in a family, and no one said it would be easy! There are no instant cures, no magic potions, that will solve everything overnight, but if you follow the blueprint for happiness revealed in this book, *From This Day Forward,* you will learn how to act toward family members in such a way that you will elicit a more positive response from them. And if you have a good relationship now, it will get even better.

Within these pages you will examine the whole panorama of family living. You'll begin with marriage and then move into the chapter on parenting. You'll take a look at families that have survived brokenness. You'll examine how young people can prepare themselves for healthy dating and courting relationships in order to avoid some of the mistakes others have made. Finally, you'll see all the pieces put together for compleat * family living now and from this day forward. As you read over the pages of this book, keep an open mind to new ideas. Look for those changes *you* can make—not those that other family members should be making!

A better way of living is available *if* you are willing to open the door to change. No matter how shattering your family problems may be at present, from this day forward you can find hope. Even if you may be teetering on the brink of separation, divorce, despair, or despondency, you can discover healing by following the blueprint. You can put into effect methods of stabilizing your life so that you will be strong enough to withstand the stresses of everyday living from this day forward. You can do this even if you are the only one in your family committed to trying!

Because I deal with families all day every day, I see much heartache and hurt beyond the wildest imagination. But I also see healing. And miracles! If your family has problems, the miracle can happen to you. You and God can make it happen.

---

* The word *compleat* has almost become a trademark for my seminars—The Compleat Courtship, The Compleat Marriage, and The Compleat Parent. So from time to time I will refer to the compleat family—the kind of family that God wants all of us to enjoy.

Chapter 2

Marriage
—Building a Happy Framework That Protects

Marriage is a great institution, only some people aren't ready for an institution yet.

Betty Ann and Raymond have been married for twenty years. In telling me about their marriage problems, Raymond put it bluntly: "I love Betty Ann, but I don't like her. You probably won't understand this type of relationship, but she tears my insides out." However, I am in tune with his feelings. Ray is committed to a twenty-year relationship with a woman who has borne him four sons. He is not considering divorce, although he can't stand her. It is simply a marriage without friendship.

Burt and Cheryl are barely existing in a marriage of eleven years. It's her second marriage and his third. Their relationship vacillates between noisy and hysterical attempts to teach the other a lesson he or she will never forget and painful silences that sometimes drag on for weeks. Both maintain sanity by minimal contact with and avoidance of one another. Each attempts to find fulfillment outside the home. Since he is a well-known professional of considerable means and status in their community and church, they plaster on cover-ups to hide the real horror at home.

Sandy and Tom had been married only six months when

their first child arrived. The presence of this new family member further unbalanced their own unstable relationship. The new father, still unaccustomed to the ways of a family man, often storms off after their fights, leaving the new bride and young mother sobbing softly. They make up after a few days, but an uneasy tension always lingers in the air—like a lull before the next storm. Their lives are a combination of unhappiness, worry, and bitterness. They feel as though they are losing their grip on sanity. They keep going only because the merry-go-round on which they are whirling hasn't stopped. But when it does, look out!

Lisa and Larry have everything money can buy. They have just moved into their dream home, which they designed and had built to their specifications. But discontent keeps creeping into their relationship. She says Larry won't listen to her and doesn't understand her feelings. Larry calls Lisa an "emotional crybaby" who doesn't make any sense. Under the constant threat of divorce, this relationship continues while each searches and finds emotional satisfaction in the arms of another.

Some harried marital partners cling to the hope that someday, somewhere, a miracle will transform their seemingly hopeless situations. Others have given up entirely. Still others go on year after weary year, merely enduring their miserable situations. How can people survive in such a stifling atmosphere day in and day out? No one ever *intends* or deliberately *chooses* this way of living. It is simply the result of not knowing any way out of the situation.

Most couples fall in love, marry, and assume the job is complete. They tend to feel that if they love each other everything else will work out automatically. But nothing could be further from the truth. A successful marriage does not come spontaneously or by chance. Instead, a happy marriage—what I call a compleat marriage—involves two people working through the small difficulties as well as the big ones.

Love and Appreciate Your Mate

From birth to the grave we all crave huge quantities of love. Love is necessary for the survival of humanity, but love—particularly romantic love and attention—frequently seems to be more important to the feminine gender than to the masculine. This overwhelming need surfaces early and remains constant all her life. During courtship a young man often seems to recognize a young lady's need for romantic attention and affection. In countless ways he shows thoughtful attention, speaks words of endearment, and bestows tokens of his affection. But once he has won the girl of his dreams, how quickly he usually forgets to continue these early attentions!

When a couple seek our advice about a faltering marriage, we frequently ask them to grade their relationship on a scale of one to ten, with ten standing for optimum happiness. The husband usually responds with a five or six, whereas his wife invariably grades the marriage at two or three! One woman ranked her marriage at minus two!

Why the discrepancy? At the risk of sounding oversimplistic, let me point out that the needs of men and women are often satisfied in very different ways. In the thinking of some men, as long as they are served good meals on time, have fresh shirts and clean underwear, and get sexual privileges when they want them, they see little wrong with the relationship. But the wife may be starved for some personal attention, caring words, and a little interest in her as a person. A lot of men regard romance as an added benefit in a marriage, but not a necessity, as it is for her.

Emotional security is the ultimate goal of many women. In order to obtain this goal, they need to experience daily expressions of romantic love. A warm hug, a lingering kiss, a sly wink, a touch of his hand, a handwritten note, a pretty flower, a well-chosen card, a surprise gift, are all indications that she is important to her husband and that he really cares.

Harry is a shining example of a man who really understands

a woman's need for emotional security through romance. When I return from giving a series of lectures without him, he'll be at the airport to greet me. On the car seat will likely be a greeting card that tells me how much he has missed me. At home I'll stumble upon a piece of candy wrapped in a love note on my pillow.

Harry makes a big production out of birthdays and anniversaries, but perhaps more important he surprises me with gifts at the in-between times—just to show he cares. On special occasions, like when another of my books is published, he'll remember me with flowers—not a dozen long-stemmed red roses, because he knows how frugal I am, but with several buds in a vase. The wink he gives me across a crowded room, the press of my fingers to his lips, the squeeze of his hand on mine, all convey "I love you and think you are special."

His caring is also translated into practical ways. Harry can sense my utter weariness and fatigue as the deadline for a manuscript approaches and things aren't going well. He's quick to say, "Honey, let's go to the coast for a weekend," or "You need a night alone with me." Other times he says simply, "You need rest. I'll cook supper tonight." Or when we collapse at the end of a rough day he suggests, "Put your feet here in my lap for a while and I'll rub them." (At this very minute we are camping by Lake Shasta in northern California. This manuscript is due in my editor's hands in less than a week, and I am typing in a motor home. Harry is at the sink, doing dishes so I can type. Now this spells Love with a capital L!)

Some men may sense their wife's distance and futile unhappiness, but they don't understand it. They are aware of their wife's constant "reaching" for them, but they don't know what she is reaching for. Some men miss the cue entirely and try to fill the void with "things." But the material goods of life will never fill the emotional emptiness of a woman who feels that her husband doesn't care about her. (And fellows, if your wife is saying things like "You don't love me" or "Do you love me?"

you're already in trouble!)

Repeated romantic attentions may seem unnecessary and theatrical to him, but not so to her. Such expressions are vital to a woman's very existence. They are often the key to her feelings of worth, her satisfaction with married life, and her sexual responsiveness. If a man feels trapped in an "iron-poor" marriage, he would do well to express romantic love consistently and thoughtfully. It may provide just the enrichment the marriage needs.

But what is a man's most basic need? According to Ruth Peale in *The Adventure of Being a Wife,* "if you want a man to keep loving you, you only have to do one thing—appreciate him and let him know you do." This bit of old-fashioned, homespun advice would save many marriages if women would only practice it. Appreciation, admiration, and respect most adequately meet masculine needs.

A bear hug after he helps you carry in the groceries and a compliment about how much you appreciate his help would make him feel that the effort was worthwhile. A sincere thank-you for taking the kids off your hands for a few hours is a must. Yet the common trend is to leave such things unsaid. How quickly we begin to take each other for granted!

Ladies, before your husband goes on parade beating his chest and making Tarzan calls, tell him how strong and handsome he looks to you. Reassure him of his sex appeal, of how masculine he is. Notice his special talents, skills, and abilities. Is he a faithful husband and devoted father? Does he provide adequate living? Does he assume leadership? Does he pitch in and help when you are behind schedule or too exhausted to carry on? Does he have a special talent that deserves recognition? Rather than taking it all for granted, compliment your husband, even if it does startle him at first. For most men, compliments are the applause that refreshes!

How do I supply Harry's need for appreciation? Since we all need physical food three times a day, I believe emotional food two to three times a day will do the trick. I begin in the morning, usually before we get out of bed. I might comment on a character trait he has evidenced. Later in the day I will appreciate his physical appearance. During the evening I might say, "Honey, that oil painting you're working on now is one of the best you've done. Those mountains look like a photograph!"

Now don't misunderstand. Harry and I are real people, and too frequently we fail and disappoint each other. We've never tried to fool anyone into believing that we live in a constant paradise of perfect marital bliss. But the fact that we try to understand each other and practice filling the other's basic needs soothes many an irritation. It gives us the courage to forgive and forget, the desire to bounce back after a struggle, and the fortitude to hang in there when the going is rough.

Whereas criticism and nagging will destroy an intimate relationship, words of love and appreciation provide a great incentive to change behavior, to be more thoughtful, to become a better person. Such affirmation of worth reinforces the self-image, generating confidence and security. Most of us would rather be ruined by praise than saved by criticism any day! During a recent working vacation trip to Jamaica we learned a Jamaican proverb that sums it up well: Marriage has teeth, and him bite very hot!

Marriage partners are always reacting to each other positively, negatively, or passively. They have the ability to build each other up, or tear each other down—to restore or deplete, to help or hinder. What about you? You can make your mate feel important, alive, and worthy, or you can make your partner feel inadequate and useless. The best medicine for healing and restoring is found in genuine expressions of love and appreciation.

Accept Your Mate

When Harry and I were dating I just knew that I had met the *perfect* man. Not that Harry was *perfect* perfect, but certainly he was perfect for me. How naive I was! Trouble erupted immediately after the ceremony, when my perfect husband began manifesting faults, a complication my youthful idealism had not foreseen. But I knew why God had put me on this earth—to reform Harry Van Pelt! With vigor and enthusiasm I launched out on my project, and total failure came as a result. With all my noble efforts to help him become the person we both knew he could become, why had my plans not succeeded?

It took almost fifteen years for the answer to come—after I had nearly destroyed our relationship. I finally learned that my responsibility as a wife was not to reform Harry Van Pelt, as noble as that may sound, but *to accept my husband just as he was!*

One of the things that I find most difficult to accept about Harry (I didn't have the intestinal fortitude to ask him what he found most difficult to accept about me!) is his total unawareness of the passing of time. He can run to a neighbor to borrow a garden tool and be gone so long I could plant the whole garden in the interim! He can be late for supper even after phoning me to say he'll be right home. Running a simple errand becomes an all-day project. I have come to realize that time means something different to Harry than it does to me. In my family of ''efficiency experts'' we were barely allowed pit stops while traveling, and since birth I have been trained to make use of every minute.

Acceptance has taught me to appreciate Harry's easygoing, relaxed nature, which allows him to enjoy frequent present-moment experiences that I bypass because of my drive to produce. Is my ''productive'' temperament superior to his easygoing one? Should I force Harry into my mold when his entire personality is geared for another speed? Fortunately, I have learned that *different does not mean wrong*. I am now free to accept his relaxed manner as an *attribute* that complements my drive to produce. Suppose both of us did have the same temperament. We would probably outdo ourselves competing to produce, or we might be so relaxed that we would accomplish nothing. Now that I understand it, I am free to admire my husband's unique, important style of productivity.

Becoming an accepting person does not mean that you will play the I-think-you-are-perfect game. No, when you embrace the concept of acceptance, it is more a change in attitude. Everyone has the capacity to make choices. We can choose to focus on strengths, or we can focus on weaknesses, irritations, faults, and imperfections. When you truly accept another person, you accept the person as he or she is, bad qualities along with the good. You recognize the negative that is there, but you choose not to dwell on it, though you could. Instead, you accept the total person, faults and all.

To be accepted in such a manner is a true gift of love. To think that someone loves you with (not in spite of) your faults is an act of love, an act of unqualified acceptance! It is also Biblical. Paul in Philippians 4:8 states: "Whatever is admirable—if anything is excellent or praiseworthy—think about such things" (N.I.V.). The opposite also holds true. If there be any negative quality, forget about it!

How frequently marriages are being destroyed by a lack of acceptance! How freely we criticize, complain, blame, put down, and nag our mates! Whether it is in the form of open criticism and belittling remarks or whether it is comprised of withering looks and a host of other nonverbals, it all boils down to unacceptance.

The most frequent method of nonacceptance that women use is nagging. God must have been aware of this female trait. Proverbs 21:9 observes: "It is better to live in the corner of an attic than with a crabby woman in a lovely home" (T.L.B.). This thought was confirmed by an elderly bachelor. When asked why he never married and assured that women don't bite, he retorted, "No, but they sure kin gnaw."

Men too can be articulate in the art of nagging, but more frequently a man will criticize rather than nag. But whatever the tactics and regardless of which sex is using them, criticism and nagging will destroy the marriage relationship. The opposite of acceptance is rejection. So unless we are actively engaged in the art of accepting our mates, we are rejecting them! We cannot ride the fence on this one.

What happens in a relationship in which husband or wife is not accepted at face value? Janice, an aggressive, outgoing person, was initially attracted to Marvin because of his slower, more conservative ways. Yet now after several years of married life she feels that he has dead-ended in his job. Her expectations for their marriage had included his rising to the top of his profession. At first she tried subtle suggestions and gentle hints. When this tactic proved unproductive, she launched into a more direct method of pressuring and coercing him into making the changes she thought he needed to make. This has driven a wide wedge between them and cut off communication, which has resulted in little sharing but much distance and hostile silence. Janice and Marvin continue to live under the same roof, yet they seldom speak to each other. The atmosphere of the home produces tremendous trauma on the children, and everyone spends as little time there as possible. Since acceptance is a basic human need, each member of the family searches for acceptance outside the home.

Perhaps through feminine insight or masculine logic you have detected areas in your mate's life that need working on. In an endeavor to make life more pleasant, you have tried to point out these areas and even ''help'' your mate get rid of these bad habits. Did you know that by so doing you are violating a basic Christian principle? The heart of the Christian message teaches that we are responsible for changing only ourselves. Jesus tells us to cast the beam from our own eye before we concentrate on the mote in someone else's. (See Matthew 7:3-5.) Someone once insightfully mused that the only nice thing about being imperfect is the joy it brings to others! But something should happen to us when we choose the Christian lifestyle. We should become more accepting, more forgiving of the mistakes of others, more appreciative of another's worth and good. If God can accept our imperfections, why can not we do the same for our mates?

Let's say that you wish to become a more accepting person. Is there a blueprint you can follow to reach your goal? I can think of two things you can do.

First, change the automatic negative response pattern you may already be locked into. In order to accomplish this task, you will have to pull out of the feeling level onto the disciplined level of mature thinking and acting. When dissatisfied with something your mate is doing, rather than responding with put-downs or criticism, change your automatic response pattern.

When your husband swears and it is extremely offensive to you, rather than withdraw or give a reprimand, do something different that would break the chain reaction: present him with a book to increase his word power. If your wife watches too much television and it is becoming destructive to your communication, rather than nag, surprise her with two season tickets to the symphony. (She'll probably go so as not to waste the money!) If your spouse is a sloppy housekeeper, present him or her with a card that promises four hours of free labor from you.

Second, begin to express your acceptance out loud. The more you say it, the more you will believe it. And the more your mate hears that he or she is accepted, the more it frees him or her to become a whole person. The more criticism and faultfinding a person must fight, the more it inhibits personal development and growth.

Although verbal acceptance is an appropriate part of everyday life when things are running smoothly, it is especially needed when we feel hurt. During periods of discouragement and frustration, we have an even more desperate need for meaningful words of acceptance—not just for the things that have been done, but a reaffirmation of ourselves as persons.

At first you might feel phony in voicing acceptance, but act from principle: Your partner has an emotional need to hear it. And the more you express acceptance, the more it will help you grow toward complete and total acceptance.

Communicate With Your Mate

Experts claim that one of the most serious problems in marriage (and one of the prime causes of divorce) is the inability or reluctance of couples to communicate. A recent survey showed that the average couple after the first year of marriage spends a mere thirty-seven minutes a week communicating. And this included such requests as "Pass the salt" and "Turn out the light." Many couples know they aren't communicating, but they aren't sure what it is they are or are not supposed to be doing.

John Powell, in his book *Why Am I Afraid to Tell You Who I Am?* describes five levels on which we can communicate. Level 5, small talk—shallow conversation, which leads to boredom and resentment in marriage; level 4, factual conversation—the sharing of information, but without personal comments about it; level 3, ideas and opinions—intimacy begins here because you risk exposing thoughts and feelings; level 2, feelings and emotions—an honest and vivid sharing of what is going on inside of you; level 1, deep insight—rare insightful moments when you are perfectly in tune with each other in understanding, depth, and emotional satisfaction. A good combination for daily interaction is to alternate between levels 3 and 2.

What levels of communication are you and your mate using during an average day? Are you satisfied with these levels? Is your partner satisfied?

Many barriers block effective speech. There are those who love to tell others what to do. There are criticizers, who put others down. There are correctors, who always have to keep the other's story straight. There are judges, who try to second-guess what you're going to say next. And there are monologuers, who have a compulsive need to carry on a one-way conversation.

Silent treatment is another barrier often used as a weapon to control the other. Both husbands and wives use silence, but generally for different reasons. When a man is silent, strong emotions such as anger or fear are usually building up inside. A woman uses silence to get even when she feels hurt or when she reaches a stage of total despair.

The hectic pace of today's lifestyle leaves us very little quality family time. To squander the little time we do have in silence seems to be a terrible waste. If you have a legitimate complaint, if you've been hurt or are angry over an injustice, why not learn to verbalize it so the problem can be dealt with in a constructive manner rather than bottling it up?

Couples wouldn't use the silent treatment so much if more trust and honesty blessed their relationship. Each partner should feel free to open up and disclose honest feelings without being put down, criticized, or made to feel inadequate. People need people to satisfy human needs. We need to talk and communicate in order to fill these needs. We all need a companion with whom we feel secure and safe from ridicule. We respond to those whom we trust. No one is comfortable living in a tomb of silence, so make it possible for your partner to open up to you.

Your listening ability can be greatly enhanced by learning the skill of "active listening," in which you *listen for feelings* behind the information. This skill is particularly useful when you sense your mate is experiencing a problem. The fact that you provide the opportunity for your mate to share problems with you establishes a closeness and intimacy that is hard to develop in any other way. Usually when you are actively listening you will be communicating on level 1. Such sharing is emotionally satisfying and develops a relationship of closeness and intimacy that is extremely rewarding.

Every marriage will encounter conflicts from time to time, but such disagreements do not have to threaten the security of a relationship if they are handled constructively. And try as you may to avoid them, you will be drawn into them. If your partner twists everything said into a personal attack, has a special gift of sarcasm, is a heavy faultfinder, makes ridiculous exaggerations, yells, even though you agreed to speak calmly, *you* can stay reasonable. You may have no control over your mate's behavior, but you *can* control your own. Choose not to argue, but calmly and quietly confront your mate. With controlled assertion, reaffirm your own thoughts and convictions. In this way you can avoid many potential arguments by choosing not to argue and by responding in a reasonable manner.

Too many couples are communicating but still don't know one another because communication stays on level 4—information about jobs, the car, the house, the kids. During all stages of married life, couples need a method whereby they can get in touch and stay in touch with each other's feelings. Time must be scheduled for this kind of communication in order for you to understand your mate and your mate to understand you.

Harry and I discovered a delightful unexpected dividend when our one luxury in life was installed in our backyard—a spa. Almost every night that we are not on the road we relax in the hot water and communicate on an intimate level. Harry is an excellent listener, and many of my female needs to have him listen to my feelings about our lives, children, and work are taken care of under a beautiful canopy of stars, summer or winter, rain or shine, in our backyard hot tub. It's a good place to solve problems in a calm manner, since raised voices would alert nearby neighbors. It forces us to keep control! Some of the greatest rewards of our relationship are intensified in our spa. Here our intimate thoughts validate each other in our relationship as a compleat couple. The world goes away, and we are compleat in each other.

What about you? Do you have a method of staying in touch with each other's feelings from this day forward? Can your relationship be called an intimate one? Does your mate know how you feel about things? Do you know how your mate feels about matters? My childhood hometown newspaper, the Tacoma *News Tribune,* once published the following typographical error: "The Kent Fire Department evacuated two families after high-tension wives were blown across their homes." Nothing is more upsetting or infuriating to a woman than marriage to a "silent partner." Take time now to get in touch with your mate.

Whenever communication between husband and wife breaks down, it will affect their relationshp with God. When the lines of communication are in working order between husband and wife, God can more easily fulfill His purpose for marriage. Honest communication allows a couple to work toward common goals and paves the way toward a truly intimate relationship between husband, wife, and God.

Understand Your Mate

From the day I married Harry I always knew our brains were different. On any given topic we could come up with entirely different conclusions. At first I thought it was because I was right and Harry was wrong. Eventually, maturity brought a proper perspective.

Recent scientific studies have revealed a basic difference between the male brain and female brain. The late physician Dr. David Hernandez, in an interview with Dr. James Dobson, stated: "The results of the research indicate that we not only have hormonal, genital, and male and female gender assignments, but that we also have brain-sex assignment. . . . Brain sex simply means that the male is different, that his brain is wired differently and functions differently than that of the female."

Dr. Hernandez went on to state that this information is highly controversial in light of certain social reforms, which contend there are no differences between the sexes. What a tremendous mistake it is to minimize the differentness of each sex, he concluded, because when we do so we actually minimize the different needs of each. Naturally, we cannot pay attention to or even begin to satisfy the needs of a partner if we are not willing to admit such differences exist.

Clearly, God specifically created the two sexes with two different sets of needs. Yet few men and women ever learn how to meet the needs of the opposite sex. Instead, they seem to assume that their partners have the same needs and respond to life exactly as they do. Such assumptions probably cause more confusion in marriage than any other single factor.

Let's take a look at a few of the female differences that men need to understand, remembering that any man who says he can see right through a woman is missing a lot!

Whereas most men derive the major portion of self-respect from their work, most women (whether they work outside the home or not) draw the major portion of their self-worth from their husbands. When a marriage turns troubled, a man usually throws more of himself into his work, but a woman has no place to which she can turn, since she draws so much of her satisfaction and security from her husband.

When a woman suffers from a lack of worth, she will likely infect the children with her negative attitudes. In addition, she will most probably begin doubting her femininity. This in turn will affect the sex life, since she will little understand her husband's desire for what she regards as her undesirable body. It will also frequently affect her homemaking ability, causing her efforts to be clouded with guilt or hatred.

How desperately essential it is for a man to understand his wife's need for self-respect and offer continual efforts to supply these needs. A man can, in part, see that such needs are supplied by encouraging his wife to have something creative and interesting to do outside the home, whether she is employed full-time or not; by securing hired help, if possible, for some of the tougher tasks like window washing, floor scrubbing, and spring housecleaning; and by providing her with the gift of listening, really hearing what is important to her as a female.

Men need to sort out their priorities and make sure they are reserving quality time for their wives. A man's ego needs can easily be met through rewarding work, and it is not uncommon for men to throw so much of themselves into their work that they neglect their families. Contrary to popular opinion, a recent survey of highly successful businessmen confirms the fact that the most successful men have put their families before their careers.

A woman also wants her husband to accept and validate her feelings. For instance, when a woman encounters a problem, she usually wishes to discuss it. Through her discussion she searches not so much for a solution but more for understanding. Since many men approach problem-solving strictly through logic, they become confused when their wife wants to verbalize a problem. But a woman perceives most problems through an emotional process, and a man who understands the process can greatly benefit by utilizing her intuition. Even though she may understand little of the issues involved in a specific problem, she can intuitively grasp the situation and perhaps offer an excellent solution. Listen to her!

Probably the most important thing of all for men to realize is that a woman wants not just the material goods that life offers but also the personal involvement of her husband. Every man must face the reality that time is passing, that life vanishes right before his eyes. Anniversaries come and go. The years disappear. Children appear and are soon gone. Everyone needs to take inventory of what is really important in life. Ask yourself: What do I want at the end of my days? If you won't be able to recall the warmth of family ties, service to others, and a sincere effort to serve God, what will you have in the end?

Similarly, many women have no more real understanding of men than men do of women. So let's look at the other side of the coin. Just as each cell of a woman's body genetically differs from those of a man, every cell of a man's body forever sets him apart as a male. He is proud of being male and of all the characteristics that distinguish him from his female counterpart. If at any time a woman belittles her husband's masculinity, she has stepped onto dangerous ground. Most women are particularly guilty of such ridicule during times of conflict. They know not to fight their husband with their fists but instead they use a tongue that is far more deadly than any weapon.

Every man dreams of a relationship so private, so safe, he can let his guard down to release his feelings freely and safely. He dreams of this kind of intimacy with a woman. But when a woman tears her man down, intimacy becomes impossible. He retreats and continues to dream of finding a relationship in which he can expose those inner thoughts that he dares to share with no one else. To belittle another is literally to *be little*.

A lot of men also have a built-in drive for position and status that most women fail to understand. A wife often mistakenly thinks that her husband works hard just to make money, but in most cases a man needs this feeling of competing and succeeding in order to fulfill his basic male needs. I have found it generally true that the more successful he is outside the home, the happier and more romantic he will be when in the home.

A man needs the solitude of his home in order to pull the tattered edges of his soul together. It is left to most wives to be responsible for the atmosphere of a home—the degree of restfulness and warmth it offers. So choose colors, lighting, and furnishings that will spell the difference between a relaxed or tense husband. Soft music, sparkling, clean furnishings, and a period of quiet provide the atmosphere that many men crave.

Paul Tournier, a well-known Christian psychiatrist, feels so strongly about the need for mutual understanding between marital partners that he says husband and wife should become preoccupied with it—lost in it—engrossed to the fullest in learning what makes the other tick; what the other likes, dislikes, fears, worries about, dreams of, and believes in; and *why* he or she feels that way. Such a purpose would lead a couple away from a troubled family directly into the benefits of a compleat marriage.

Support Your Mate

The young couple who had come to consult with us had been married only five weeks, yet they were talking divorce! The problem, according to her, was that he wasn't pulling his share of the load. She had listed twenty-one family tasks that needed to be done each week. She was doing eighteen. Together they were doing two. And he was doing only one.

Obviously they had both contributed to this setup—she by taking control and he by allowing it. In effect, they had a parent-child relationship.

At the close of their first session with us he commented, "It's really hard to make love to your mother."

Fortunately, they stuck by their relationship and worked out the many questions they had failed to ask or answer prior to their marriage. You see, few couples prior to marriage ever discuss who is going to be responsible for what after marriage. Who will do which tasks around the house? If she works outside the home, will he assist with the housecleaning? Since she has as much earning power as he, will he still make all the financial decisions?

Traditional role patterns in today's society are being challenged, which leaves Christian couples who wish to follow Biblical guidelines tremendously confused. The patriarchal pattern (husband-dominated relationship), the matriarchal society (wife-dominated relationship), the coleadership role (equal control), and the power struggle pattern (fighting the other for control) all have their limitations and liabilities.

There is a better way—a supportive relationship, in which both partners willingly relinquish the power to dictate and control. Neither demands his or her own way, insisting on unquestioned obedience. Rather, each shows a readiness to negotiate and compromise until common ground is established.

The husband leads in certain areas because of his competencies. She leads other areas because of her capabilities. Both parties, however, agree that the husband will assume the responsibility for overall family leadership in accordance with the model found in Scripture.

Such "mutual submission" is based on Ephesians 5:21, which reads, "Submitting yourselves one to another in the fear of God." I infer from the counsel that the marriage relationship is not as one-sided as many might have imagined, but rather that each partner operates with a willingness to adapt when the need arises.

Marriage requires a good deal of mutual submission, flexibility, give and take, and compromise. Here's how Harry and I utilize the mutual submission principle in our home. Harry is definitely president of the Van Pelt Corporation, but as any well-trained executive would do, he checks out his plans and decisions with his vice president. I, as vice president, have certain areas of responsibility that I carry out on my own because of my capabilities and inclinations. Others I check out with Harry. We hold frequent meetings between us to discuss plans and objectives. He respects my opinions, abilities, and experience, and he wants my maximum input in family matters.

During times of conflict Harry tries to be understanding of my position and does not make unreasonable demands on me. He tries to be sensitive to my needs. This does not mean that I will always get my own way, but I can always count on him to deal fairly with me. He recognizes my rights in each issue. I reciprocate, respecting his needs.

I've noticed that sometimes a woman wishes her husband would assume more leadership in the family, but unconsciously she hinders him by bucking his every idea or by criticizing his faltering attempts by saying "I told you so!" when failure occurs. If you are married to a weak leader, step aside and stop making decisions if you ever expect him to assert himself. Through appreciation you can encourage him to try again.

Couples who function in a mutually supportive manner under God's guidance have fewer arguments and less fighting. A natural peace settles over the home. Power struggles vanish, and a closeness results that would not be possible any other way. Together, as they back each other up, their roles enrich their relationship and make their marriage more fun and enjoyable. Through such an example children learn a natural respect for home, school, church, and society as a whole. When the homes are in order the community, the church, and the nation can function as they should.

Sexually Fulfill Your Mate

Healthy sexual satisfaction results from harmony in other areas of marriage. As a couple learn the meaning of genuine love, as they practice accepting one another at face value, as they work at the art of appreciating one another, as they learn the principles of effective communication, as they unravel individual differences and preferences, and as they adapt to a workable supportive relationship of mutual respect and trust—only then can they expect a mutually satisfying sexual experience.

And it takes time for this adjustment to occur after marriage. Many couples think they will attain instant sexual harmony. But it takes time, understanding, patience, study, experimentation, and open discussion before a couple can master the ultimate in a fulfilling sexual relationship.

A problem can arise when one partner desires intercourse more frequently than the other. While both sexes exhibit variations of desire from person to person and from occasion to occasion, men hunger for sexual release more consistently than do women because of the overabundance of semen that collects over a period of days in the seminal vesicles. Studies indicate that a healthy man's semen builds up every forty-two to seventy-eight hours, producing a pressure that needs release. When the needs of one spouse are greater than the other, happiness demands compromise. Husbands have no right to demand intercourse at their every whim, but many wives are willing to go out of their way to express their love for their husband once they understand that a man's need for sex is more than just having "sex on the brain."

A woman responds to a man in direct proportion to his ability to fulfill her emotional needs. By failing to create an atmosphere in which his wife can respond, a man can deprive himself of the sexual pleasure that is important to his happiness. He may wonder how she can say that she still loves him and yet deny him what he wants and feels he needs most. But when things are out of balance in the sexual department, a husband might well look to himself: There are not as many lukewarm or frigid wives as there are husbands who fail to meet their wife's emotional needs first.

Lovemaking is a deeply emotional experience for a woman. She is stimulated by the amount of romantic love her husband has shown throughout the day. She tends to consider each lovemaking encounter a moment of profound love. If her husband seems to take their sex life for granted, she may feel deeply hurt and offended. She needs reassurance, not because she is vain or seeking flattery, but rather because she withdraws instinctively from sexual encounters devoid of love and caring.

Women do not need to achieve an orgasm every time in order to enjoy sex. Many women can participate in sexual relations, not achieve orgasm, and yet feel fully satisfied. A husband should not *demand* that his wife achieve an orgasm. She might lose interest in sex altogether, or she might begin to fake an orgasm.

Another simple thing that many of us forget is that what turns a man on is not what turns a woman on. A woman needs to hear tender words and to experience feelings before she can respond in the bedroom. Women want little attentions, kind words, concern, and gentle caresses in order to set the mood. A husband who thinks he can merely walk into the bedroom and expect his wife to "turn on" with no preparation doesn't understand female sexuality.

To a great extent, when it comes to sex, men are the initiators, women the responders. But women must have something to respond to. Even an inhibited woman can be responsive if her husband woos her gently, slowly, patiently, and creatively. A song some years ago revealed the key to unlock her heart: "Try a little tenderness."

I have discovered that fatigue is one of the main hindrances to a woman's interest in sex. After she has struggled through a grueling eighteen-hour day, sexual intimacy may be the last item on her mind. But a loving wife will sort out her priorities so that sex doesn't languish in last place. The wife who considers the sexual aspect of her marriage to be important will reserve time and energy for it.

What do men want and need? A survey of a large group of men listed an unresponsive woman as the biggest turnoff. A cold, uninterested woman irritates men most during sex. Few husbands will complain about a passionate, creative wife who responds to his advances with enthusiasm. The only portion of the sexual experience a man enjoys more than ejaculation is the satisfaction he derives from an amorous wife who finds him sexually stimulating. Sometimes, however, a Christian wife does not see creativity and responsiveness as part of her demeanor. These women might be surprised to learn that in a survey I conducted on sexual attitudes, 65 percent of the husbands wanted more interest, response, and creativity from wives. Only 35 percent felt satisfied with the status quo. Although it may not be necessary to cavort in baby-doll pajamas and high-heeled boots à la Total Woman, routine sex does become dull sex. A new look in the bedroom, an intimate candlelight dinner for two, a new place or time, might give routine intimacy the boost it needs.

Men seek sexual contact for a variety of reasons beyond love and affection. A frustrated and discouraged man, when he returns home from work, may seek intercourse as a release for his pent-up emotions. His desire may spring from sadness or loss or from pleasure over an accomplishment. Few if any of these experiences have any direct connection with his wife, yet he seeks a sexual experience with her because of the feelings generated by another sector of his world. Sex comforts a man. Affection comforts a woman.

God designed that sexual relations—unhampered by selfishness—be exciting, enjoyable, and fulfilling. Good sex, then, comes as the end result of a satisfying personal relationship. If sexual problems plague your marriage, don't look for the answers in your sex life itself, but instead scrutinize the quality of your total relationship.

Have Fun With Your Mate

So far I've outlined principles that will take genuine work and self-discipline to put into practice. But unless you add the dimension of fun, enjoyment, and delight to your relationship, life may turn into a desperate struggle.

From our earliest years of marriage, Harry and I have found time, despite hectic schedules, to include activities that will enrich our married life—an evening at a motel, picnics at a favorite spot by a creek, a hand-in-hand walk beside the brilliant blue surf, or a relaxing drive. We religiously engage in fun activities on a weekly basis for the sake of our marriage.

On a recent weekend, to add an element of fun and variation, we sought refuge on the California coast. After checking into a motel in Monterey we went out for supper. Pure happenstance led us to a pizza parlor that claims the best pizza in town along with homespun entertainment. What fun we had listening to old songs rendered by five lively "troubadours" brandishing their guitar, ukulele, mandolin, violin, and washtub bass viol. An unexpected delight! The next morning, rather than breakfasting (we were saving our calories for a fancy dinner later on), we took to the seashore, where we relished clear blue skies and the fresh breeze off the sea. We playfully perched ourselves on the large rocks and tossed crackers to undaunted sea gulls. A chipmunk sporting an appetite arrived on the scene to check out the menu. Quite a crowd gathered to watch the fun we were having with all our new "friends."

A drive along the coast and a late-afternoon dinner at a favorite Mexican haunt provided a perfect ending to the day. From our vantage point we observed a group of scuba divers emerge from the waters while spouting whales surfaced in the distance. This respite from the grind and fog of everyday life provided the change of pace we needed. It revitalized our relationship and provided a healthful tranquilizer. It made each of us feel special, young, and in love all over again.

How about you? Are you fun to live with? Would you like to live with you? Make today and every day from this day forward a happy day for yourself, for your mate, and for your family. Come up with a surprise. Share a funny story. Plan ahead for a special occasion. Discover a new and interesting place. Smile. Laugh. Take time to play. Find a way to have fun with your mate. Make your married life just as enjoyable as can be.

Worship With Your Mate

Almost every married couple expect to have a supremely happy marriage. But few experience it. Why? All too often it's because they have not discovered the missing dimension—the dimension that helps them deal with conflicts and incompatibility. You see, the ideal husband-wife relationship is not just a commitment between two persons, but a triangle consisting of husband, wife, and God. As husband and wife draw closer to God they also draw closer to one another. Adding the spiritual dimension, then, takes the kind of relationship described here and transforms it into a powerhouse of strength. "Except the Lord build the house, they labour in vain that build it" (Psalm 127:1).

It is a beautiful experience to reflect on the possibilities of worshiping the One who can save you from sin, take away your guilt and shame, and promise you eternal life with Him. How can you find this kind of experience so that you and your mate might share the worship experience? Naturally, it is important that you have personal devotions and attend church regularly. But how often do you and your spouse pray aloud—*together?* Praying out loud to your heavenly Father is one of the best means of improving communication between two people. A marriage can be completely transformed when a couple regularly seek the Lord in prayer together.

Here's a suggestion for a new way of praying that could prove to be a tremendous blessing in your life. Each night one person should begin "share prayer" by praying for a specific subject. The other partner in turn also prays for the same subject. Then the first partner prays for the next burden on his or her heart, and the other prays for the same thing. They continue until the one who began no longer introduces a new item to pray about. The next night it is the other person's turn to initiate the topics for prayer.

By praying for each other's concerns both of you before too long will be concerned about the same matters. After a few weeks of "share prayer" you won't be able to remember who had the burden first. It won't even be important, for you will each be closely identifying with each other's burdens!

One marriage counselor reached a stalemate with two couples he was counseling, so he asked them to try "share prayer." The first couple began the program that very night, and within a month they announced that they no longer needed counseling. The Lord had worked out all their problems! The other couple refused to try such a method of praying, and even after many months of counseling they were still at a deadlock.

When a couple learns how to pray together, they will have discovered an important preventive measure against marital difficulties. Morning and evening prayer were once an established institution in homes. Today, the number of couples who go month after month without prayer is probably astronomical! Yet most of them are professed Christians. According to a survey of Christian marriages taken by Dr. Pitirim Sorokin, of Harvard University, there is only one divorce in 1,015 marriages where Bible study and prayer are practiced daily.

I would like to share a personal testimony to the stabilizing force of the spiritual dimension in marriage. During our early married years, Harry and I consistently experienced numerous problems. We were young, naive, and unlearned in the disciplines of married life. We felt as though we had been thrown together to work out problems on our own, and we weren't doing very well!

Harry was training for, and subsequently entered, the ministry during this time when we were "rocking" along. We went to church, read our Bibles, and did all the good things Christians are supposed to do. But things continued to worsen.

Had it not been for our faith, we might have thrown it all away, figuring that what we had together wasn't worth saving, that it might be better for all of us involved to go our separate ways and not "torment" each other any longer. But the closer we faced the reality of separation, the more we wondered how we could disgrace our church and sin against our God. The faith we had been reared in held us, and it would not let us go. Ultimately, it became a stabilizing factor. Then I began learning the principles that make marriage work successfully. As God led, I followed. It was difficult, but change did come about.

Had it not been for our Christian faith, when the going got rough we would have scrapped our marriage. Today we are stronger than ever in the Lord's love and our love for each other. Harry is my pride and joy.

What lies ahead, then, is up to you. You can stay where you are or you can look up. You can say, "Lord, I can't," or "Lord, I will." Success will not come merely through your own efforts, but much can happen when you link your efforts with divine power from this day forward as you attempt to follow the blueprint to family happiness.

Chapter 3

Parent
—Furnishing the Rooms With Happy Children

Husband, wife, and children form the world's greatest team. Whether that team wins or loses depends largely upon whether husband and wife practice human love.
—Rhoda Lachar

The Johnsons are a family of five—Mom, Dad, and three school-age children. Dad sees himself as "boss" of the family. In a domineering, dictatorial manner he demands adherence to the rules that he sets up, with no input from his wife or the children. He obtains obedience through fear, not respect. As a result of the constant overcontrol that Dad enforces, the children are losing their ability to make proper decisions, since they are robbed of any opportunity to think for themselves—Dad controls everything.

Small misbehaviors in the Johnson family lead to major incidents of bawling the child out. Then an uncomfortable silence pervades the home. Mr. Johnson, already in a stressful condition, now finds himself even more upset over the complications resulting from his behavior, so he sends the child to bed early; the child thereby loses any opportunity for positive interaction with Dad. Mom withdraws as she helplessly realizes that her attempts for a pleasant evening have been absolutely futile.

When one of the Johnson children misbehaves, Dad begins a half hour stern lecture followed by a severe spanking and hours of resentment on the part of both parent and child. Mr. Johnson sees his role as boss and disciplinarian only—not as a loving husband and father who provides a role model for his boys to follow in the future. As a result, there are few opportunities for positive family interaction.

Mr. Johnson rarely takes his wife and children on family outings. When he does, the occasion turns stressful because of his constant reprimands, warnings, and many angry outbursts. A steady barrage of criticism and correction follows the Johnson children wherever they go. They hardly know what kind words, hugs, affection, and encouragement to do better are all about. The children secretly vow that someday they will break loose and retaliate against this man. Feelings of insurrection lay dormant, waiting to erupt during the teen years. It's only a matter of time.

Let's look in on the Smiths, a family of four—Mom, Dad, and twins, age 8. John and Geri Smith see themselves not as bosses but as team leaders. John doesn't undermine Geri's authority, and Geri doesn't undermine John's. When they disagree over a disciplinary matter they do so privately and come across to Mike and Mindy as a united team.

When the twins misbehave, as they frequently do, they are punished. Mom and Dad explain the reason for the punishment so that the experience can serve as a lesson for the future. The parents also make sure the twins understand that it was the *behavior* that cannot be tolerated, not the twins. The punishment will likely be followed by tears, but the Smiths hold Mike and Mindy to reassure them they are loved, so that the children understand they are loved and cared for in spite of their bad actions. The goal in the Smith household is not so much for immediate, instantaneous obedience as it is to help the children learn inner controls and self-discipline. Hence, Mom and Dad watch their timing when they attempt to teach their children obedience. They look for opportunities when the twins are ready to listen, not just when Mom and Dad feel the urge to teach.

John and Geri Smith have open communication between each other and encourage the twins to be open also. If Dad comes home in a grouchy mood, Mike might say, "You're sure grouchy tonight, Dad," without fear of retribution. Dad would likely respond, "You can tell, huh? Yeah, I had a rotten day. I'm beat. I don't want to take it out on you or anyone else in the family, so you better let me unwind a bit."

The Smiths nurture their marriage relationship by taking time for each other without involving the children. They also have family time. One night a week after supper they play games, pop corn, sing, play ball, swim, or engage in an activity they all enjoy. The Smith family places a high priority on having fun together.

Troubled parents will most likely produce troubled children. Troubled children grow up to be emotionally disturbed adults, who perpetuate more troubled families. Through compleat parenting emotionally healthy, happy, productive children emerge and grow up to be responsible members of families and society. It is essential, then, for parents to be competent before they tackle their important work.

It may be more difficult today to rear well-adjusted children than ever before, but it is not impossible. Parents who take the time to prepare for this awesome responsibility will be richly rewarded. If changes need to be made, these changes must begin with the parents. If you respond differently to your children's behavior (or misbehavior), then their conduct will change. And this is what the following guidelines are all about—helping parents to improve their attitudes and interaction with their children.

Please don't feel guilty about, or blame yourself for, past mistakes. Considering that most of us have had little or no training in child rearing, we generally do a remarkable job. Besides, guilt feelings do not produce competent parents. Don't dwell on your past failures. Don't rebuke yourself for what you should have done. Instead, from this day forward reinforce your own self-worth by recalling your successes as a parent. Perfection in parenting is an unattainable goal. Improvement, however, is realistic and necessary for building stronger families.

Reflections on Your Child's Self-respect

Feelings of worthlessness have reached epidemic proportions and are almost universal. On every hand we witness the results of those who feel inferior. Why do so many children grow up disliking themselves? Parents have not understood how to structure a child's environment so that self-respect can be built rather than destroyed.

How is self-respect formed? It begins in the tender years of childhood. For most parents, it won't suffice to say a plain No to a child when his or her behavior infringes on the right of others. Instead, typical parents feel they must continue: "No, you naughty child, that was a *bad* thing to do. You *always* do the wrong thing!" Words such as *naughty* and *bad* serve to form that very image within the child—an image he will subconsciously seek to live up to. Subjected to a constant barrage of this kind of talk, along with nonverbal disrespect or emotional neglect, a child begins to grow up being ashamed and dissatisfied with self. Feelings such as "I am no good" begin to grow.

At least three factors must always be kept in mind when discussing the development of the self-image: (1) Self-respect is a learned response to the total combination of life's experiences; (2) self-respect can be earned by doing something worthwhile; and (3) self-respect must be experienced—a child can sense his parents' love and care by whether he is made to feel worthy.

Charlie Brown, star of the ever-popular Peanuts series, has *learned* that he is inferior to others. Put him next to a drinking fountain, and he knows it will soak him with spray. He has failed at earning self-respect because he is unable to do anything worthwhile. On the pitcher's mound he is a total and complete flop. Since he has no friends and no one cares whether he lives or dies, he does not experience love and caring, either. He consistently fails in each of life's endeavors. Experience upon experience compounds to drench Charlie Brown with a sense of inability to measure up. Just as Charlie Brown's down-in-the-mouth response to life has been *learned*, so are your child's negative or positive feelings of worth learned. The more positive the experiences you provide for your child, the more positive the feedback he receives from you, then the greater the chances of your child *learning* that he is a person of worth and adequacy.

Loving your child is not enough. Your child must *feel* your acceptance of her as a person—*feel* that you appreciate her individual worth whether or not she accomplishes anything great in life. For this reason I insist that love is not the greatest gift a parent can give a child. *Self-respect* is the greatest gift. A child cannot experience or return love until he or she first learns self-respect.

Our society has created a false value system that effectively destroys human worth. If a child is good-looking, he or she has a great advantage, because our society highly prizes beauty. Adults tend to respond favorably to a cute child and overlook an unattractive child.

Another critical factor by which we measure the worth of an individual is one's intellect. A child with intellectual deficits may be able to survive the early years with self-respect intact, but when that youngster reaches school, the picture changes drastically. Now he will be measured and compared with the others in his grade, and it won't take him long to discover that he can't measure up to his brighter friends. Since approximately 22 percent of all children in the United States are in the slow-learner range, these youngsters leave the first grade with ingrained scars of inadequacy.

Other factors such as physical deformity or oddity can almost ruin a child's life. Financial or social deprivation, being brought up in a single-parent home, having alcoholic parents, having a mentally or physically disabled sibling, belonging to a different race or religion, or being crippled through unloving relationships are all factors that can haunt a person all through life.

You do not wish your children to be laughed at, put down, called names, ridiculed, ignored, or snubbed by others. However, you can do little to prevent it. Your job as a parent is not to protect your children from every hurt in life, but rather to prepare them to accept the inevitable hurts and nobly rise above them. You can teach your children to allow the words and reactions of others to destroy them, *or* you can teach your youngsters to grow emotionally stronger through successfully handling problems.

Parents can usually tell when a child feels rejected, because fear of failure and criticism dominates his emotions. Accusation and reproach will cause him to justify his existence by creating arguments for his own defense. Such fear and uncertainty exhaust a child emotionally and drain him physically. Therefore, a rejected child exhibits certain signs or clues: (1) hesitation on minor decisions; (2) withdrawal or fantasy (he may drift into a world of make-believe); (3) a cool or nonaffectionate attitude; (4) repeated deliberate misbehavior such as excessive biting, hitting, kicking, habitual lying, or stealing; (5) abnormal attempts to please; (6) habitual easy crying—crying or pouting when he doesn't get his own way; constant complaints like "They don't like me" or "They won't play with me"; (7) tension—shown through bed-wetting, nail biting, head-banging, stuttering, or nausea.

Fortunately, a child's self-concept is not forged for all time, although once established, it is not easily changed. Since feelings of worth are learned, earned, and experienced rather than inherited, attitudes toward oneself can change when one encounters a positive experience with people and life. If your child lacks self-respect, work to provide a loving, accepting atmosphere. You'll find that as a result of your consistent effort, your child's self-concept will change over a period of time.

Children who already have a tendency toward developing a negative self-image can be helped to develop a more positive image with the right kind of encouragement from caring parents and others. Redirect negative traits into more positive qualities for which the child has talent. Any child who is different than the group or the "norm" in any way—if he is too short, too tall, too slim, too heavy; wears glasses; has protruding teeth or ears; has any distinguishing features; or in any way differs from what is important to his peer group—will need what I call a *specialty*.

A specialty will counterbalance his weaknesses and help him capitalize on his strengths. If your child can do something well, it will make up for those times when his peer group rejects him. And at some time in every child's life he *will* receive rejection. For example, if you have a son who is small for his age and not good in sports (both size and sports skills are important to peers), direct him to carpentry, sailing, music, or photography. By the time your child is 8 or 9 years old, he or she should have developed a skill or ability as a specialty. Then when your child feels rejected by others, he will hurt, but he can also say, "OK, you don't accept me. You're laughing at me and making fun of me. But I can do something you can't do." Specialties must sometimes change with the age and maturity of the child, but every child needs one to carry him over the rough spots of life.

Why not take an inventory of the emotional climate in your home? Have you created an atmosphere of acceptance in which your child can nurture positive feelings of worth? Have you conveyed acceptance in terms your child can understand? Does your home contribute to the building of self-worth, or toward the destruction of it? Must your child make you proud before you can accept him? Does your home contribute equally to the self-worth of each family member?

Happiness truly is feeling good about yourself. Learning to

live with your children so that they are confidently glad they are who they are bequeaths to them a priceless legacy. The greatest gift you can give your children is a healthy self-image. Then they can understand the depth of meaning found in the word *love*.

Communication Designed to Build a Well-adjusted Child

Most parents assume that in order to develop their child's character, they must tell him what he is doing wrong. They consequently load their speech with preaching, admonishings, and commands—all of which convey nonacceptance. Their verbal communication consists mainly of negative criticism.

The American Institute of Family Relations reports the results of a survey on negative and positive comments to children. Mothers kept track of the number of negative remarks they made in comparison with how many positive comments they made to their children. The survey revealed that the mothers made ten negative comments for every positive comment! In other words, 90 percent of their total communication was negative!

Under a barrage of harangues, belittling, and put-downs, little people soon find it safer and more comfortable to keep their thoughts and feelings to themselves. Criticism makes them defensive. So to avoid further complications they enter a silent world at home and choose to communicate only with their peers and other well-chosen friends.

Unless parents learn "the language of acceptance" they will never be able to know what is going on in the hearts and minds of their children, and there will be no basis for a warm relationship between parent and child in which the child feels accepted. One of the easiest ways parents can convey this kind of acceptance is by saying, "I understand what you mean," or "I see what you are saying."

Of course, parents who want open communication with their children must prepare themselves to hear some rather threatening things. What good are you as a parent if you want to hear only the good and the pleasant? Young people need to share their joys, yes, but they also need someone with whom they can share their problems, their heartaches, their fears, their failures—someone who will not fly to pieces and shout incriminations.

Often when children share emotions with us we proceed to tell them how they should or should not feel, as though our statements of logic can erase their feelings. Bill Gothard, of Basic Youth Conflicts, tells the story of the little boy who said, "My daddy made me sit down. But I'm standing up inside." Telling a child that she shouldn't feel the way she does will not make her feelings go away. Negative feelings are a fact of life. We cannot live from day to day without conflicts, and human conflicts engender negative feelings. By telling children to calm down, not to be angry, or to stop feeling the way they do, we push them from us. Our words tell them that a part of them—what they are feeling—is unacceptable and that they are terrible for having bad feelings.

When emotions surface, parents should accept the feelings and provide acceptable outlets such as active sports, hobbies, music, drama, or even old-fashioned work. When your child experiences a real problem or emotional turmoil, you should listen for feelings, not facts. Restate these same feelings in an understanding manner. At this point you must restrain the natural parental impulse to solve the problem or tell your child what to do. By assisting your child to express the problem aloud, you will be helping him learn how to handle negative feelings in a positive way. Your child will also learn that his feelings are safe with you, and thereby you are establishing a solid relationship with him.

Dr. Haim Ginott, in his best-seller *Between Parent and Child,* also stresses listening for feelings (page 18). His classic example revolves around a young boy's first visit to nursery school. "Who made those ugly pictures?" the boy asked.

His mother tried to shush him, but the teacher broke in and

explained, "In here you don't have to paint pretty pictures. You can paint mean pictures if you feel like it."

Then the boy asked, "Who broke this fire engine?"

Mother answered, "What difference does it make to you who broke it? You don't know anyone here."

The teacher responded, "Toys are for playing. Sometimes they get broken. It happens."

In each case, Dr. Ginnott says, the boy actually wanted to know what happened to children who painted poor pictures or broke toys. The mother perceived the words and questions, but not the feeling behind them. The teacher picked up the child's feelings behind the questions and then reassured him.

Thirteen-year-old Michael unloads on Dad how upset he is. "That coach was so unfair in the game today!"

Without making any judgments or suggestions, Dad feeds it back to him. "You're really upset over something that happened with Coach Simpson."

"Upset is the understatement of the year," continues Michael. "You should've seen what he did when I . . ."

"I can understand how you must feel when something like that happens," Dad continues, staying with the active listening approach.

Rather than analyzing the situation and giving a logical explanation to justify the coach's behavior, which would further frustrate Michael, Dad relied on active listening responses, which allowed his son to feel that he had someone who understood his problem. Michael felt free to open up and express the full story.

The parent who will listen with appropriate variations of active listening, along with a tell-me-more attitude, will provide the sounding board that every child and family member needs from time to time. Once private feelings are exposed, however, you must restrain the urge to give advice, criticize, blame, or make judgments. This is not the time for that.

Here are five ways to improve your listening skills:

1. Maintain good eye contact. Get on eye level with your child. Turn off the television, put down the paper, and forget about cleaning the house. Focus your full attention on your child.

2. Show interest. Sit attentively. Raise your eyebrows. Nod your head in agreement, smile, or laugh when appropriate.

3. Use phrases and gestures of agreement, interest, and understanding. Your child wants to know that you understand what is being said.

4. Ask well-phrased questions. Give encouragement for sharing by asking questions that illustrate your interest.

5. Listen a little longer. Just when you think you are through listening, listen thirty seconds longer!

If communication in your family has broken down, it is up to you to do something about it. If the lines of communication are open, do all within your power to encourage such vital exchanges, for it is an unhappy home that lacks interaction. Keep little differences from growing into big ones by resolving them while they are tiny and can be handled. Don't let your children keep their anger toward you or others buried inside to fester and erupt in later years. The Scriptural admonition "Let not the sun go down upon your wrath" (Ephesians 4:26) holds for children as well as parents. Heal the wounds while they merely are scratches and easy to mend.

The Rewards of Discipline

Most parents recognize early in the parenting process that they must limit their child's activities and teach him to control his behavior. They sense that if they do not begin early, their child may be well on the road to Tyrantville!

At this point a common mistake parents make when beginning the discipline process is to label their child "bad" when in fact the little tyke is not bad at all. For example, a mother who has an intense headache might tell her son that he is a "bad boy" for slamming the door, when in reality it was little more than childish exuberance that caused him to slam the door. The child's actions may have caused Mother a problem, but this does not mean that the child is bad. When parents become angry because of the inconvenience of misbehavior, resenting the extra work the child causes and the price of parenthood, the child perceives he is a burden rather than a blessing.

If a child feels respected when he is corrected, he will not lose respect for himself even though he may have done something very wrong. He will feel bad about his mistake but believes he can overcome the problem. If you attack his self-respect for poor conduct, you will rob him of his feelings of worth. The less your child feels loved during these times, the more motivated he will be to defy your authority or look for other deviant methods of getting back at you. The more you meet your child's basic need for self-respect during the disciplinary procedure, the less your child will show defiance. Discipline and self-respect are intrinsically bound together.

I'd like to mention five avenues to a well-governed child.

1. Gain and maintain respect. The respect that a child maintains for his parents is in direct proportion to the respect he'll hold for the laws of the land, the police force, school authorities, and society in general. Respect, however, is a two-way street. If Mother belittles Jimmy in front of his friends and Dad is sarcastic with Jimmy, they should not expect respect in return. Parents who gain and maintain their children's respect during the early years will generally have respect from their children when they are teenagers. And parents must realize that if they aren't worthy of respect, neither is their religion, their morals, or any other standards they espouse. The Ten Commandments teach a child to "honour thy father and thy mother." One child, when asked to recite the Decalogue in class, responded, "Humor thy father and thy mother." Both are great ideas!

2. Set limits. Whenever two lives cross, it is necessary to establish well-defined boundaries in order to maintain friendly relations. Your child needs to know what you will permit and what you will prohibit. Keep specific limits down to as few as possible, and make them reasonable and enforceable. Then as your child matures, withdraw or modify the limits you have previously established. When a child is aware of the limits, he usually doesn't get into trouble unless he deliberately asks for it.

3. *Teach your child to reason as well as to obey rules.* The long-range goal of parents is to teach a child to guide his own behavior, to make good decisions, to reason clearly about choices, to solve problems on his own, and to plan ahead. When a child understands the consequences of his behavior, he can make better decisions for himself in the absence of his parents. Parents should teach a child to reason out the consequences of his own behavior.

The rules made should be short, easy to remember, and stated positively instead of negatively. Try "You may turn on the television after you finish your homework," instead of "If you don't get your homework done, you can't watch TV." Rules should also specify exactly what you want done as well as the consequences for noncompliance. Be specific. When the rule states the details of what has to be done, the child cannot make excuses for doing half the job.

4. *Speak once, then follow through with action.* If the kids come to the table with dirty hands, you needn't rerun the same old lecture: "How many times do I have to tell you to wash your hand first! You act just like pigs!" Simply remove their plates and serve no food to those who have dirty hands until after they have washed. The next time it happens Mother doesn't even need to mention why she isn't serving some people. Control maintained through empty threats is poor control. It contaminates the parent-child relationship. Parents who rely on such methods often sigh, "He never hears a word I say!" Why? These children find talk a bore and become "mother deaf." How much better to speak once in a calm, rational manner and then follow through with action. Action will bring about

obedience much more quickly than words—and with much less wear and tear on Mom and Dad!

5. *Balance love and control*. Extremes are rarely good, and this certainly holds true when disciplining a child. The extremely authoritarian, permissive, possessive, or mixed-discipline parents (one harsh, the other lenient) are all extremes best avoided. A child learns rapidly how to respond to each parent and adjusts behavior accordingly.

It would be convenient if we could rely entirely on respect, setting limits, rules and reasoning, action, and natural consequences to discipline children, but this is not always sufficient. At times punishment is necessary. No children are so well-behaved (at least no children we ever sprouted) that no punishment is needed.

There are three common methods of punishment: (1) deprivation—removing something from the child that is important to him; (2) isolation—sending a child to her room, standing him in a corner, or sitting her on a chair; and (3) spankings. If the child's misbehavior does not directly challenge your authority, the first two methods are probably most satisfactory.

Spankings, however, are sometimes necessary when other resorts fail, though they are not a cure-all for every type of misbehavior. But when a child directly challenges your authority, displays an attitude of direct defiance, or in effect says, "I will not do as you asked me to do," he needs to be dealt with in a strong way. If a spanking does become necessary, carry it out in such a way that it will spare the child's self-respect.

I believe that most parents resort to spanking too frequently. If you find yourself constantly falling back to the use of your hand to control your child, perhaps you should reevaluate your entire disciplinary system. Remember also when dealing with a child that a little pain will go a long way. Before you spank, make sure the child understands clearly why he is being spanked. He must know what rule he violated and that the result of disobedience is punishment. When his tears have subsided you can tell him how much you love him, how much he means to you, how much God loves him, and how much it hurts God to see any of us disobey His laws.

It takes real character on the part of parents to teach obedience. But parents cannot take a popularity poll every week to see how they are doing in the eyes of their children. Discipline is amost a twenty-year project. But if parents do their part, along with the church, the school, and society, then over those twenty years the child will gradually develop inner controls.

Character Under Construction

Character. The very word evokes a myriad of nuances and diverse meanings. When we say that a child possesses a fine character, we are referring to moral excellence. If we were to say that a child has a pleasing personality, we mean that she is well-mannered, attractive, likable, or good-natured. The word *character* comes from a Greek word that means "to engrave." It is the mark of a person—the pattern of traits within one's lifestyle.

All the attitudes and facets that go into shaping a child's character are *learned*. This makes it rough on parents, since it puts the responsibility of character development squarely upon their shoulders. But because the results of building character do not appear immediately and too many parents define character solely in terms of whether a child obeys or not, the task of developing character is frequently neglected or carried out in a haphazard manner. Perceiving no immediate results from their efforts, parents frequently do not pursue this task as enthusiastically as they should. But it is the long-term value of the results that should be stressed rather than the *immediacy* of the results. Successful Christian parenting does not demand immediate results of one's labor, but patient consistency.

The atmosphere of the home is very important to the child's

budding development. The troubled home, where parents show a lack of respect for one another, where there is quarreling, jealousy, dishonesty, power struggles, or strife of any kind, regardless of how carefully the parents may try to hide this, will most likely produce children suffering from some distortion of development. The main ingredient for a child's character development, then, is that parents themselves be whole persons and that they learn to relate to one another in the family with mutual love, respect, and appreciation. The young child "absorbs" his character inclinations unwittingly from those around him. "Caught, not taught" is the byline here.

How can parents develop consistent growth patterns in a positive direction? How can parents get a child to brush his teeth regularly, make his bed, pick up his clothes, or stop whining or dawdling? By associating pleasant reactions with what is right and unpleasant reactions with what is wrong. A child will learn to repeat acts for which he is rewarded. Reward is a powerful determinant of behavior.

Unfortunately, many parents unwittingly utilize reinforcement to train their child to be obnoxious! While shopping, Mother meets a friend and stops to visit. Little Marty asks for something in a quiet voice. Since Mother is busy talking with her friend, she doesn't respond. Marty's voice gets louder and whinier until Mother can't tolerate it. She interrupts her conversation to listen to Marty, and when she does, she reinforces loudness and whining.

Three types of reinforcers are especially important to parents. *Social reinforcers* involve the parent's behavior—the tone of voice, words of praise, attention, smiling, touching, and being near. *Activity reinforcers*—such as games, reading aloud, running errands, watching TV, having a party—can all be used as reinforcers. Such things as points, stars, stamps, charts, and money fall into a third realm of *token reinforcers*, which can be saved or accumulated and exchanged for a long-range goal.

A variation to the point program is the grab bag. This

involves purchasing inexpensive objects from the toy store and filling a bag with them. When a child performs the appropriate behavior, he should be rewarded with a social reinforcer first (a hug, a wink), and then allowed to pull out one object from the bag.

Negative behavior should generally be ignored, because even negative comments about a misbehavior may reinforce it! Learn to reward the positive behavior, and remember that unreinforced behavior will eventually disappear. How difficult this is to believe during a recurrence of obnoxious behavior when you "go nuts" trying to get your child to take out the garbage and then on the way back he'll bring you a flower!

Any activity that absorbs a large portion of a child's time will influence his character. Since the average child watches nearly three hours of television daily, it exerts a major influence on character. Television can become a "school for violence" and advocate mediocre values (or worse!). It insidiously cuts out family communication, produces callousness toward human suffering, and reduces time for play activity. Can you see why it's important to develop self-control and parental control of our offspring so that televison does not constitute a steady daily diet?

Enter Project Television. In Project Television you set up a weeklong log in which you, or your child if he is old enough, will carefully enter the date, the name of the program, and how long the program was watched. During the week you take notes on program content, which means you will have to monitor all programs during that time. Ask such questions as What kinds of programs is my child watching? Cartoons? Situation comedies? Science fiction? Westerns? Which shows should be rated positively? Negatively? For what reasons? What values are being taught? What kind of language is my child hearing? How much violence is being depicted? What values is my child learning from this particular program?

After a week of such a project go over the results of your

findings with your child. Next, have the child rank the programs he wishes to watch—from his most favorite to his least favorite. In some cases it may be necessary to work out an agreement to limit TV viewing to two hours a week.

Other forms of entertainment are just as destined as television to destroy elements of character. These include various movies, books, magazines, forms of music, and places of amusement. The solution lies not in merely banning these items, but in providing positive, enjoyable substitutes.

Another important aspect of character development is religious training. Your child's religious experience will be greatly influenced by the experiences of everyday life. This fact must not be overlooked by parents who give religious instruction. If the instruction is to become part of a child's life, it must first be a part of the child's parents' lives.

A child's visual image of what God is like may include a blend of information from pictures she has seen and stories she has heard. Her concept of God may change from a compassionate facial expression to a vengeful one. His concept of God as a father will be influenced by the relationship and attitudes developed with his earthly father. The child's idea of sin will be shaped by his experiences of guilt and remorse—by hurting others and then facing the resultant feelings of regret following punishment. His ideas of forgiveness are affected by his parents' ability to forgive him. Forgiveness is very difficult for a child to grasp if his parents do not extend forgiveness to him. To a great extent parents stand in the place of God to a child.

You do not have to be perfect in order to maintain the respect of your child. But your family will lose respect for you if you are pious at church or in front of friends but the opposite when no one but family members are present.

One young father rose early to have time for personal devotions one morning. He was alone in his study before the rest of the household was up when a sleepy-eyed daughter wandered in. Irritated with the interruption of his thoughts, he ordered her to get out. She ran tearfully to her mother and asked what Daddy was doing in his study. "He's trying to learn to love the people at his office." Love the people at the office? When you can't be loving to your own family? Such behavior forfeits the respect of the watchful child.

One minister has noted after years of observation that the church's best young people come from either consecrated Christian homes or non-Christian homes. Homes in the mediocre category just don't produce dedicated Christian young people because of the inconsistency present. Youngsters can pick at words, but they have a hard time disputing a consistent example of good living.

What about church attendance? Is it a factor in family living? What effect does regular church attendance have on a couple, their marriage, and the children born to them? Researchers have conducted numerous studies to determine the divorce statistics among families who never attend church, as well as among those of differing religious faiths. All statistical data gathered to date show that mixed-faith families (in other words, those who do not worship together) experience trouble sooner after marriage, seek separations sooner after the wedding, and experience more divorce than do couples who worship together.

One study by Paul Landis, researcher and author, explored the question of who it was that took the responsibility for the religious training in homes of mixed-faith couples. In more than a third of the cases the child was exposed to both faiths, sometimes by one parent, sometimes by both. In a few cases the child was actually taken to both churches in turn. Students, looking back at the mixed-faith marriages of their parents, were inclined to feel in general that it had been a serious handicap in their home lives. Another study showed that six out of ten children from mixed-faith homes ended up rejecting all religion entirely.

On the other hand, religion is an asset to families who share the experience. Without a doubt, worshiping together makes a significant contribution to the success and stability of a family. The unhappiest families are those with no religion at all, closely followed by mixed-faith families who fail to share each other's religious interest. This leads to one important conclusion: *The worship experience contributes to family stability and success when it is shared by all family members*.

The Greeks had it right. Character is an engraving. What kind of permanent inscription is now being deeply etched into the very heart and soul of your child?

The effort you expend in good parenting will rarely be appreciated by the world as a whole, but in the judgment all will appear as God views it, and He will openly reward those who have prepared their children for His kingdom. It will be seen then that one child, brought up in a faithful way, is worth the effort expended. It may cost tears, anxiety, and sleepless nights to oversee the development of a child, but it's part of the blueprint for family happiness. If you have worked wisely unto salvation, you will hear God say, "Well done, thou good and faithful servant."

Chapter 4

Remodeled Families
—Caution: Major Reconstruction in Progress!

*Nobody's life is smooth and easy. Everybody
has ups and downs. We've got to expect that.
And since we should expect it, we should also
be ready for it, prepared for it. Then when it
happens we accept it naturally, as a challenge, as a measure of the stuff of which we
are made. Indeed, we may even be eager to
try ourselves out, to discover how capable we
really are.*
—Louis Bisch, M.D.

The newspaper ad read: "Diamond wedding rings, value
$300. Will sell for $175. Candlelight wedding dress, size 12,
$75. King-sized bed, $60." An interview with the person who
placed the ad revealed that it had been a storybook wedding. The
first four years were great, but in the fifth year things began to
sour. He was going to college and working nights. She was just
as involved with her work, and they didn't have much time to be
together anymore. Soon they began to drift apart. Attempts on
her part to talk about what was happening were met with
opposition. He couldn't see that anything was wrong. After a
year of such behavior, they gave up and headed for the divorce
court.

That was four years ago. She was terribly broken up at first,
but time was healing the wounds and she was now doing
fine—in fact, felt optimistic about the future. She had survived!

But if she was doing so well, why had she waited all this time to sell her rings, the wedding dress, and the king-size bed? A long moment of silence followed before she explained that her ex-husband had just remarried. Suddenly she realized that she never could wear the rings again, nor could she look at the dress without crying. Her story ended.

A half hour later she called again with one more thought. In a faraway voice she began, "I think people give up on marriage too easily. I know I did on keeping a promise that I so cherished. Although I'm optimistic, I think about my marriage constantly, and I have regrets that I didn't put more effort into saving it. I guess I just didn't stop and think what I was really giving up."

Divorce is painfully destructive and, as a cure, worse than the "disease" itself. The previous chapters have been preventive in nature—aimed at helping people establish healthy relationships prior to the time serious problems might develop. I have tried to offer how-to information with many practical solutions for common family problems. Now we'll look at life from a different angle. Many times problems, ranging in intensity from mild to serious, already exist in some families. Since many households today are quaking from within as a result of extensive wear and tear, a message is needed that can bring healing to families already in a state of brokenness and crisis. I see a great need for both positions: preventive (to resolve problems before they actually occur) and curative (to help solve problems already present).

If you are suffering in a state of brokenness, hurt, grief, or heartbreak over something that has already occurred in your family, take this as a message of hope and encouragement. You may or may not find an instant cure for your difficulty. Some problems have no cure. *But we can learn to live with the scars*.

Is Divorce the Cure for an Ailing Marriage?

You clutch your divorce papers in your hand. At last you are free, free, free! Now you can put the past behind you and look to the future. Or can you?

Today many people herald divorce as a remedy for "bad" marriages. Yet the joy people expect to experience after their release from a relationship that failed to measure up to their expectations might be described as a bottomless pit rather than the rainbow after the storm. Long-term feelings of bitterness, resentment, and rejection usually result.

If the idea of divorce has ever crossed your mind, you owe it to yourself to consider seriously whether divorce is the cure for an ailing marriage. And don't rely on the opinions of a few friends, the advice of a divorced acquaintance, the fantasies of what life could be like if you were only free of the bondage that now chains you to unhappiness, or books like *Creative Divorce,* which attempt to con people into believing that unprecedented opportunities lie just ahead. When considering an experience as sacred as marriage, you must confront the unavoidable facts about life after divorce. The truth is that divorce is not the perfect solution for even a long line of domestic problems. Excruciating pain usually accompanies the breaking of a relationship as intimate as marriage, and it is more intense and complicated when children are involved.

One reason divorce is so devastating is because of the rejection that accompanies it. To the same degree that falling in love is exciting, falling out of love can hurt. Divorce is a painful process. Even if you are the one who initiates the divorce, or were not at fault, or did not desire the divorce, or were the "innocent party," or tried your best to keep the marriage intact, this does not mean that you can escape the emotional crisis that accompanies divorce.

Most people agree that divorce is more painful than the death of a loved one. In death the relationship is over and done with. Only memories linger on. But in divorce a relationship still exists—especially when children are shared. Many couples have said to me, "If children are involved, divorce is never over!"

Try as they may, most people can't escape their former partner. More than half of all divorcees admit that their ex-partner is the first one they call in cases of emergency. Holidays can become the most psychologically torturous time of the year, with Thanksgiving and Christmas bringing on major migraines. Every continuing encounter is a reminder of a failure and the rejection you have suffered. There lingers a wondering question about whether the ex-partner might return. Former in-laws and friends further complicate the issue. And when a recently divorced person enjoyed a regular sexual relationship within the bounds of holy matrimony, what is he or she to do now? It is interesting to note that 12 percent of all divorced persons continue their sexual contact with each other during the first two months after divorce.

The issue of whether to try marriage all over again must also be faced. Statistics show that 80 percent of all divorced and widowed women will eventually remarry and that percentages are slightly higher for men. However, second marriages have a higher failure rate than first marriages and continue to worsen for third and fourth marriages. Furthermore, the one out of fifteen couples who attempts to reconstruct a relationship with the same partner have a less-than-average chance of success.

Isn't it strange that we have made so many technological advances in our society in recent years, yet we still can't teach families to live in harmony under one roof? Divorce is a sad enough indictment against the general population, but it is infinitely more appalling for committed Christians who claim to have the power of the gospel at their fingertips.

However, once couples learn the basics of interpersonal relationships as they apply to marriage, troubled relationships can be turned into happy ones! Divorce is *not necessary* in the vast majority of cases when a program of study, application, and change is begun by one or preferably both, partners!

How can I make such a sweeping statement? Harry and I had just finished conducting a Compleat Marriage Seminar. People were pressing us with thanks when a couple we had not met before approached us rather shyly. With tears streaming down their faces, they said, "Well, you have just put two lawyers out of business!" I had an inkling regarding what they meant but encouraged them to continue. "The divorce papers were all signed, sealed, and delivered," the man responded, not the least bit embarrassed by the very evident tears running down his face. "But there's going to be no divorce in this family! You've shown us a blueprint for happiness." The two of them hugged the two of us, and we all wept with joy because another family had been rescued from the very brink of divorce. It *is* possible.

Divorce is rarely the cure for an ailing marriage! The cure to the majority of troubled marriages is found in education prior to and during marriage, creative counseling, and reliance on divine power for solutions. *Divorce invariably creates more problems than it solves.* Research confirms this fact of life. A lawyer explained to one divorce-seeking husband the cooling-off period, reconciliation efforts, and child-custody investigation that are all part of a Wisconsin divorce. Finally the would-be divorcé sighed, "Forget it. I can't stay mad that long!" In a study that followed divorcing partners for a five-year period after the divorce, only 25 percent appeared to be able to cope adequately with life. Fifty percent muddled along in a "barely coping" capacity. The remaining 25 percent failed to recover or else they looked back with intense longing to times before the divorce, wishing the divorce had never taken place. Divorce hardly settled anything for these persons, but it did supply them with an entirely new set of problems. Ah, the insight of hindsight!

Divorce statistics are rising even among Christian families. Within many Christian circles there is no difference between the divorce rate within the church or without. A sad indictment! Christian parents who divorce must answer some serious questions regarding their children. Not only must these children face the dissolution of one home and the creation of a new one with all the necessary adjustments, but these children often have some serious questions about the religion of their parents. "Why didn't God save our family?" "Why didn't God answer my prayers to keep our family together?" "Why didn't God help you and Daddy work out your problems?" Any child confronted with such a dilemma could become seriously disillusioned with Christianity and question whether it is worth it to establish a relationship with a God who seemed unable to help parents during a time of need. Countless parents have thus become stumbling blocks to their own children's eternal salvation. And children from divorced families are themselves more likely to divorce later in life. A high price indeed!

If you are considering divorce, you owe it to yourself, your partner, and your children to consider the following blueprint for family living.

1. Seriously study Scriptural references against divorce. Read Matthew 5:31, 32; Matthew 19:3-9; Mark 10:2-12; Luke 16:18; Romans 7:1-3; Malachi 2:13-16, RSV; and 1 Corinthians 7:10-17.

2. Study how to have a successful marriage. Read books, attend seminars, and exhaust resources that can show you practical solutions to common problems. It appears that most efforts to "save" or do something about a failing marriage occur too late. Experts recommend that couples should attend a marriage seminar or see a qualified counselor as a matter of routine every year, rather than waiting until they are in deep waters. And yet how frequently Harry and I face the public's attitude in our Compleat Marriage Seminar: "We don't need a seminar. There's nothing wrong with our marriage!" Surveys indicate that most divorced persons not only would have preferred to stay married but also wished they had acted sooner to seek outside help.

3. Seek professional counseling. If you are experiencing difficulty now, seek the help of a qualified counselor. Seek help at the first sign of trouble rather than waiting until there is a deep chasm separating you from each other. The average couple wait seven years before seeking help with a problem. By that time the problem is so complicated, the habit patterns so deep, the hurt so intense, that it becomes much more difficult to solve.

4. *Accept responsibility for changing your own behavior*. If you stand at bay, saying, "I'll change when you do," you'll get nowhere. Commit yourself to change whether or not your partner agrees. Your partner, regardless of the circumstances, is not 100 percent responsible for the problems in your marriage. It takes two to create most problems.

5. *Pray for patience, instruction, wisdom, and courage as you seek to salvage your relationship*. Make sure during this time that you have placed every aspect of your thinking in God's hands lest you be lulled into thinking that you are following His will when, in fact, you are doing the opposite.

6. *Bury all thoughts of divorce*. The fact that you look to divorce as a solution makes it more likely to happen. Banish divorce from your mind. Resist any angry verbal threats of divorce. You may not mean it, but pride may block you from backing down from what you said in anger.

Regardless of the problems you face, heed the flag of caution. Look before you leap. Divorce in all its ugly, shadowy specter for the uninitiated is even more ugly and trauma-ridden after you've been through it. If you are in a situation where divorce cannot be avoided, if you have become a victim of divorce through no choice of your own, if you were divorced before you became a Christian—in other words, if you are the unwilling victim of circumstances—do not allow these circumstances to defeat or permanently discourage you! Use your past experiences as stepping-stones to personal growth. Such an approach will provide a powerful modeling example for your children and others as to how faith works.

Do Broken Homes Produce Fractured Children?

Two weeks before her divorce was to become final, a friend

who had become like a sister to me called to update me on the status of things. "How are things going?" I queried cautiously.

"Great. Just great. I have peace for the first time in years. Things couldn't be better," she responded.

Our conversation then drifted to 6-year-old Bernie, whose custody she had voluntarily given to the father. She admitted concern. "He's doing better than he was. He had a lot of stomach pains, so Henry has been taking him to a psychologist. The sessions have helped. The pains in his tummy and the nightmares are subsiding."

I felt like screaming at her, "What your child needs right now is not a psychologist, but a mother *and* father *and* a secure home."

Divorce will always have a damaging effect on children, and it is time for adults to stop playing the game called Denial. Yes, children are resilient, but this does not mean that they are not seriously affected by the breakup of their homes. Even children who show no outward symptoms during or after the divorce can be affected. The time has come for a realistic appraisal of the effect of divorce on children.

According to Dr. H. Norman Wright, psychologist and imminent Christian family counselor, research illustrates that a child of parents who are going through a divorce experiences the same stages of grief he would if a parent had died! Furthermore, few children are warned that a divorce is about to take place. About 80 percent of all children are not prepared in advance of the event. Even when the news is broken gently, the child experiences shock, depression, denial, anger, fear, and a haunting obsession that he might have been responsible.

Children respond differently at various ages:

1. Toddlers (2-4 years of age) frequently regress to more babylike behavior. Potty-trained youngsters need diapers once again. They become more passive and dependent, even wanting to be fed. They tend to suffer from irritability, whining, crying, fearfulness, sleep problems, confusion, aggressiveness, and tantrums. It is this age group that is the most seriously affected by divorce.

2. *Young children* (5-8 years of age) also regress in their behavior to bed-wetting, loss of sleep, nail-biting, irrational fears of being abandoned, and a deep sense of sadness. In one study 50 percent of the 5- and 6-year-olds seemed able to handle the crisis after a period of time, but 25 to 50 percent continued having rather severe symptoms and yearned for their fathers. Some authorities believe this to be the most critical period for children to experience divorce.

3. *Older children* (9-12 years of age) experience primarily anger—not necessarily anger at the parent who initiated the divorce, but frequently such children choose a scapegoat outside the family to hate. The spiritual development of the child is most critical at this point and rejection of parental values most likely to occur. "I don't want anything to do with a religion that can't help my parents solve their problems."

4. *Teenagers* (13 years of age and up) seem somewhat less affected than younger children, probably because they can more easily understand the reasons for divorce. Nevertheless, they still can be deeply traumatized by the divorce. The more distant and removed the adolescent is from the divorce proceedings, the better she is able to handle the situation.

In *Children and Divorce* author Archibald Hart cites a 1978 study from England which showed that children from divorced families have shorter life spans and more illness than do children from homes untouched by divorce. The children also leave school earlier. In New York City, where teenage suicide leads the nation, a study found that two out of every three suicide victims came from broken homes. According to psychologists, boys seem to suffer from divorce more than girls do, probably because in our culture boys have been taught not to express their emotions. This denial of feelings affects men even into later life. Boys are also expected to be stronger and tougher than girls.

When a divorce is hotly contested, where there are custody

battles and children are used as pawns or go-betweens, the effects can be worse. The child's normal capacity to cope is more seriously impaired. Furthermore, when a couple claim Jesus Christ as their personal Saviour, the confusion and bewilderment resulting over their inability to solve their problems in spite of the spiritual resources available to them is devastating to the child's belief system.

The effects of divorce on children are not always short-lived either. Studies on the subject by Onalee McGraw reported in *The Family, Feminism and the Therapeutic State* show that 37 percent of all children whose parents divorce suffer depression even as long as five years later. Such behaviors as chronic and pronounced unhappiness, sexual promiscuity, drug abuse, petty stealing, alcoholism, acts of breaking and entering, poor learning, intense anger, apathy, restlessness, and a sense of intense, unresolved needs manifest themselves. Another 29 percent were making ''appropriate developmental progress'' but continued symptoms of sadness and resentment toward one or both parents.

In most cases, say the experts, it takes three to four years before a child can pull herself together after a divorce. This means that if a child is 4 when the divorce occurs, she will be 7 or 8 before the effects subside—almost half of her 8 years being lived in the awesome shadow and aftermath of divorce.

Sometimes parents feel they are doing the child a favor by providing a new or more peaceful atmosphere. Only 10 percent of all children of divorced parents report any feelings of relief. And despite feelings of relief, they still have difficulty adjusting to the divorce. Furthermore, most children, even those from very troubled homes, would go to almost any length to get their divorced parents together again. Many children from broken homes share a common fantasy—a miraculous dream that their parents will reunite. Such a fantasy often lives on for years.

Perhaps you are wondering if I feel a very troubled family should stay together just for the sake of the children. No doubt there are extreme situations of physical or sexual abuse, where the effects of staying would be as serious as the effects of divorce. In most cases, however, *it is preferable to save the existing family whenever possible rather than to opt for divorce*. This choice, of looking for ways to solve a troubled family situation, is far preferable for all parties concerned. And the theological implications of divorce for a Christian couple have not been considered yet!

The Single Parent—Can One Parent Do the Work of Two?

One of the greatest social phenomena in family life today is that at present more than one million American children live with only one parent. Furthermore, many children who now have two parents have had only one in the past or will have only one in the future as a result of separation, divorce, or death. If the present rate continues, almost one in two of all children will live in a single-parent household before they are 18.

Parenting alone is, quite frankly, more difficult than parenting with a partner. What were shared responsibilities before must now be maintained alone—supporting the family, maintaining the car, entertaining friends, remodeling, repairing home appliances, housecleaning. Then there are all the tasks related to child care itself—nurturing; discipline; listening; setting limits and rules; settling quarrels; transporting children to school, music lessons, and meetings; helping with homework; family worship; caring for clothing; plus countless other tasks. If you were to ask a two-parent family if both parents kept busy all day, both partners would insist that they had full-time jobs whether inside or outside the home. Now, however, one partner must shoulder the entire burden. Under such circumstances, management takes on new meaning and should receive utmost attention.

Whereas parents care about their children, single parents have a special reason for cherishing their children—in most cases it is all that remains of their "family." Divorced single parents frequently hope that successful parenting can in some way compensate for the marriage failure. The widowed often commit themselves to their children to show continued fidelity to their former spouses. Children give special meaning to the lives of single parents. In a way, it is easier for single parents to focus on the child's needs because they don't have to divide time between a spouse and a child. But in so doing some parents tend to become overly protective. They may also become overly concerned if their child seems troubled. Single parents usually have cause for concern if there has been upset in the family because of separation, death, or divorce. Indications that the child is not doing well include excessive misbehavior, insecurity, attention-seeking behavior, or declining grades in school.

One of the biggest problems that faces single parents is child care. Who will watch the children when the parent is not at home? Surveys show that most single parents are not satisfied with their present child-care arrangements and go through a succession of possibilities before settling on one. Summers and school vacations present special problems in one-parent homes. Living near grandparents or relatives is often helpful.

Recent statistics show that about 55 percent of single-parent mothers work outside the home, and another 12 percent are actively looking for work. Single mothers, more than other working women, need the nonmonetary rewards that work outside the home offers. It provides them with the financial support needed, yes, but it also provides them with a social life and much-needed self-esteem. Single parents who work full-time frequently worry about what their absence from the family will do to their children and suffer feelings of guilt because of it, even when the child evidences no signs of problems. Single fathers seem to carry less of a guilt load about working and also being a parent than mothers in the same category.

Financial problems piled on top of everything else can

compound the problems that single parents face. Single parents who are forced to live on a reduced budget should not shudder at having to discuss finances with children. Level with them. Be calm and matter-of-fact. Above all, don't feel guilty for having to turn down a request for a new bike or whatever.

Single parents with small children meet up with special problems. As much as the parent may cherish the child, he or she may not be able to escape the child, which can lead to irritation as a result of incessant claims on parental time and attention. Naturally, this occurs in two-parent families as well, but single parents are particularly vulnerable because of the frustration of the situation—work problems, home responsibilities, insufficient funds, and many other stresses unrelated to the child. The parent wants to do the things all good parents do but fails, and so guilt feelings escalate.

Once the child reaches school age, parental guilt feelings connected with child care tend to decrease. But new problems surface as the child enters a new social world—sports, games, birthday parties, sleep-overs, and church activities.

To face the challenge, single parents, more than married parents, need a support system and companionship outside the home. Children alone just can't fill the void. The single parent needs outside help because he or she has no one inside the home to turn to for support. Without a partner, all responsibilities must be borne alone, and all emergencies present a double challenge. Friends, neighbors, relatives, singles' groups, and the church can all provide portions of the support system—the single parent's lifeline. It becomes the stability factor—the key to a single parent's emotional well-being as well as to the child's.

If being a single parent has any consolation, it might be the opportunity to draw closer to one's children. Since there is no other adult in the household and no one else to distract time or attention, it becomes natural for the parent to discuss with children all the events of the day, plans for the week, menus, and many other things.

This too can be carried to extreme. In one case that came to my attention a young mother invested too much in her relationship with her 4-year-old. He could do whatever he liked, whenever he liked. He had no set bedtime and could often be found running around at 11:00 P.M. Mom checked all menus with him. If little Jamie wanted chocolate milk on his mashed potatoes, chocolate milk on his mashed potatoes he got. Single parents will want to exercise common sense during such times!

It may also be easier for children to talk with a parent about their problems, friends, and school when the parent is alone. But talking to children is not the same as talking to an adult, though it is better than talking to no one! And single parents need to be cautioned not to rely on their children for sympathy or support during times of stress. Children often assume that they are to blame or attempt to assume responsibility for helping the parent solve the problem. Children cannot become emotional substitutes for a missing parent.

Another benefit to single parents is that there is no one with whom to disagree concerning discipline. There is also less opportunity for children to "divide and conquer," since they often have to assume more responsibility and thus may grow up a little faster.

Spiritual training should be given top priority in the one-parent home. Particularly is this true for a child whose father is no longer in the home. This child has most likely not had a lasting relationship with a father. Since parents stand in the place of God in the eyes of their children, it might be difficult for the child to relate to a heavenly Father. A loving, nurturing mother can help a child form a proper concept of God by her own example, by teaching the child God's Word, and by allowing him to observe godly male models.

If you face the prospect of rearing your child alone, keep in mind that your child's basic needs are exactly the same as every other child's needs. The thing that is most different is that you must see that these needs are satisfied without the help of a mate.

But God has not left you helpless, even though you are alone. God can and will guide you step by step with or without a parenting partner.

Managing well as a single parent stems from a combination of having an adequate support system available and a positive attitude. Parenting in general will naturally produce its own kind of stresses, but single parents should recognize the contribution they are making—alone! Few other things in life are as rewarding as rearing well-adjusted, responsible children.

The Blended Family—Will It Work?

Estimates indicate that by the year 1990 stepfamilies will outnumber biological families in the United States. A leading family authority has stated that stepparenting is five times more difficult than any other kind of parenting!

I agree. The most confused, angry, bitter, and uncooperative families I encounter are those who are trying to blend "his kids," "her kids," and sometimes "our kids." In one particular instance a very troubled family came for help. The new stepfather blamed their unhappiness on his wife's 16-year-old daughter. He angrily growled at one point, "I married her mother, not her!" I pointed out that when one marries a woman with minor children it's a package deal. The children come with the mother.

Contrary to popular opinion, remarriage will not automatically solve all troubles—particularly when children are involved. One study of two thousand stepchildren, most of whom came from divorced homes, found a greater amount of "stress, ambivalence, and low cohesiveness" than that which occurs in primary families. The study also pointed out that it was more difficult to be a stepmother than a stepfather and that stepdaughters had more trouble adjusting to the new family than stepsons. Obviously then a stepmother will have to work harder at developing a relationship with a stepdaughter.

Children between the ages of 12 and 18 present the most

challenging problems. Very young and college-age children adjust most easily, with 6- to 12-year-olds falling somewhere in between. But whatever the age, parenting his, hers, and our children presents some unusual challenges.

Yet frequently single parents rush into relationships without the knowledge or approval of the children involved! One very angry couple sought my counsel regarding their tangled relationship. They had met at a Christian singles' retreat and "just knew God had put them together." The man married "my dream wife" just three weeks later, without having met the three minor children for whom he would now become father figure and disciplinarian. The relationships among these family members never blended, and another remarriage succumbed to divorce. Many times the adults could make a go of their relationship, but working out the difficulties of integrating the children into this new union failed dismally.

Both the parent and the stepparent must "get their act together" *first* so that their expectations coincide. Once agreed, both parents together should then discuss the matter with the child so that the child gets the clear feeling that the stepparent is part of the permanent "team."

Even though behavior expectations may have been discussed prior to marriage, parents can expect opposition from the children. During the first few years after remarriage, children tend to recognize only the natural parent's right to discipline. The children will test and retest the limits set by the stepparent. It is part of a child's need to explore the limits of any new relationship or situation, so the sooner the stepparent makes his presence felt and shows the child that he is there to stay, the sooner the child will accept the reality that his former family is gone (either through divorce or death) and accept the new situation. But be patient during the adjustment process. Most authorities agree that it takes 2 to 3 years for the average child to work through the stages of recovery, and some are now saying 7 years.

In a home where there has been no divorce and remarriage, either parent can resolve problems created by a child and administer punishment when it is called for. If the punishment is unfair, the child generally forgives readily whether or not the parent asks for forgiveness. But not so in the blended family. Instead, the stepparent questions his own right to discipline; the natural parent questions whether the stepparent is being fair; and the child questions the stepparent's rights.

When discipline cannot be shared equally with both parents concerned, the quality of the family life will be seriously affected. Two broken family units have not joined to form one new unit. Think of it from the child's point of view. When we marry, we do the selecting. But in the parent-child relationship, there is no choice.

Stepparents should mentally prepare themselves, in most cases, for initial feelings of resentment rather than love. Instant love should not be the goal of stepparents. When one becomes a stepparent, it is important to remember that the child has already sustained a loss through death or divorce—a loss that makes him extremely vulnerable to hurt. He has just come through a devastating emotional drought, which affects his behavior and frequently causes him to act worse than normal. The stepparent often misinterprets the misbehavior to be a rejection of him when this is not so. And the stepchild who only visits on occasion may never feel any "love" in the real sense of the word. Someone has suggested that the word *love* should be stricken from the stepparent's vocabulary. Instead, it might be better if the stepparent and child formed a relationship of respect that might blossom into affection with time.

Many times a stepparent thinks that the child's attitude toward the new parent will change over the months. As the child gets older he or she will think of the new parent as a real mother or real father. Nothing could be further from the truth. Whereas children automatically grow up loving their parents, there is nothing automatic about the love between a child and a stepparent. Actually, the stepparent and child are in competition for first place in the other parent's life. Both want to be more special than the other.

No one can force a child to love a stepparent. But both parents can make the child understand that even though the stepparent is not the real parent, he or she will be carrying out all the functions of a parent, and whether the child loves the new parent or not, the child must obey. This procedure will take courage and strength on both parents' part, but the sooner it is done, the stronger the relationship will become.

The situation most likely to present pitfalls is when the rejected partner remarries before working through feelings of bitterness toward the previous spouse. Such "unfinished business" allows anger and hostility to flow over to the children. Contrary to popular belief, a stepparent can build a relationship with stepchildren most easily when the children are on good terms with their natural parent.

Becoming the stepparent to the child of a divorce may be much different than living with a child who yearns for a new parent to fill the void left by a parent who died. The longer the child has lived in the single-parent home after the death of the parent, the more rigid her memories tend to become and the more difficult the adjustment may be. The child will likely expect the new parent to take up where the old one left off, and this just isn't possible.

Every child in the newly formed family should feel a part of the family as soon as possible. The child needs to know he has a special "place." Even if the stepchild only visits on weekends or holidays, it is still necessary to arrange a place that belongs only to him—a bed, a drawer, certain possessions. In the blended family, where two sets of children are merged together providing a space all his or her own for each child becomes even more important. One mother who moved her two children into the home of her new husband and his two children said, "All the children have been forced to do some adjusting. The children must share bedrooms. My oldest daughter wants a bedroom of her own, and my husband's children are whining, 'Whose house is this, anyhow?' ''

The entire stepfamily needs to find a common ground, an activity, a sharing of jobs, that can bring them together. It might be weekend camping, a sport enjoyed by all, a love for birdwatching, or perhaps leading church activities together. But it needs to be something that will help the family members form bonds of friendship with one another. A child can be loved by his biological parent, but to be loved by someone who *choses* to love you is something quite different and brimming with exciting potential.

A happy ''blended family'' is possible from this day forward where the adults are mature, patient, and persistent, and when the love of God is consistently demonstrated during the blending process and beyond. Always remember, however, that the most important relationship exists between husband and wife, not between parent and child. When the husband-wife relationship is functioning at peak efficiency, the parent-child relationship has a better chance of succeeding. Yes, blending *can* bring mending.

Surviving Hurt to Become a Compleat Person

The vast amount of traveling that Harry and I do brings us in contact with many people who suffer from tragic pasts. Some of the stories we've heard haunt me yet. On one occasion a woman cautiously approached me and asked for a private appointment. When we got together she related an almost unbelievable tale of horror to which she had been subjected. At age 6 she watched her mother murder her father. He had returned home after a night of drinking, and fearing for her daughter's and her own life, she shot him, rolled his body in a rug, and heaved it into the trunk of the family car. She then drove to a nearby lake and attempted to dispose of the body. The mother was later arrested for her crime and sent to prison. With no father or mother to care for her, the little girl went to live with Grandma and Grandpa. Grandpa sexually molested the little girl for the next five years.

What is your story? Maybe you too have been a battered or an abused child. Maybe you are the victim of divorce, desertion, abuse, or the death of a loved one. Perhaps you could tell a story that would make someone else's hard times sound like child's play.

When we have been hurt or a problem surfaces within our families, we have several alternatives from which to choose. We can find a scapegoat upon whom we can heap all blame. We can escape into a world of alcohol or the euphoria of drugs, or we can retreat into silence. We can run away and hide. Or we can look at the situation as honestly as possible and say, "What can I do to remedy or improve the situation?"

True, you cannot wipe out the past, nor can the harmful effects on you or your family be erased. But you can turn to a blueprint for rebuilding a solid, happy future.

Sometimes you might get to thinking that no one else in the world has experienced what you have gone through. You might conclude that because no one else has walked in your shoes, other people can't understand you. But this simply is not true. Granted that you are a distinct individual and that your case may be unique. Granted that others would need to walk in your moccasins for many miles in order to understand completely the uniqueness of your situation. But even then, many family problems share similar aspects. And although no one on earth can solve all the problems you face or immediately take away all your hurt, you can be helped toward change if you can be challenged to action.

It takes courage to make changes—to admit that you may have been a part of the problem, to stop blaming others even when you are a victim, to stop nursing your hurts, to face courageously other family members in a responsible manner and work through complex issues of rejection, confronting what is fair and what is not. All of this can become bearable, however, when you recognize that life is full of challenges. The price may be high, but it is possible to work through chaos. Even though all of your problems may never be solved, you can look forward to a continuing process of growth and improvement.

Persons who are hurting emotionally frequently won't *do* anything because they don't *feel* like it. Yet such persons would likely *feel* better if they could begin by *doing* better. In other words, feelings can be changed by taking appropriate action. Two questions concern us: Do we begin acting better when we feel better? Or do we feel better when we act better? Both approaches might be effective, but usually we respond to the latter method more rapidly. Yet how difficult it is to discipline our actions and our feelings! The apostle Paul states, "I do not understand my own actions. For I do not do what I want, but I do the very thing I hate" (Romans 7:15, R.S.V.).

If we are going to follow the blueprint to happiness in family living, we must begin changing ourselves. Yet how many of us are divided within ourselves! We are restless, dissatisfied, tormented—tearing apart our own world, poisoning our own environment, and hurting the ones whom we love the most. Such behavior produces troubled families and, eventually, troubled human beings.

Look at us! We are a mass of contradictions. Sometimes we are loving and kind; other times cruel and hateful. Sometimes we will stand by loved ones; sometimes we fail them in their hour of greatest need. At times we act with great concern and wisdom; other times we behave with merciless foolishness. We long to be close to our families, yet we drive them away through our responses or we recoil when they approach us. How can we expect anyone else to understand us when we don't understand ourselves?

Obviously, we need a plan, a blueprint for surviving the hurts of the past so we can progress toward becoming fulfilled persons regardless of what has transpired prior to this time. Let me share with you a plan I have formulated, a plan that has assisted many who seek permanent renewal and satisfying personal growth. I hope it will be your blueprint for happiness from this day forward.

1. *Commit yourself to God every morning.* There is a transforming power that lies within reach of every human being. This transformation cannot be accomplished by calling on the powers that lie within yourself. But God's power to change you is infinite! And yet that power lies mostly untapped by human resources.

The one-time superficial prayer of "God help me" won't do. In order to change deeply ingrained habit patterns, you will need to maintain an hour-by-hour connection to heavenly power. God will always be present to assist you with every problem. He will provide the strength to make the right choice in every situation. A favorite prayer of mine comes from an old Virginia Negro spiritual: "O Lord, please prop me up in all my leaning places."

2. *Release the hurts of the past.* You can choose to keep alive every agonizing, torturous detail of the past, or you can break free. If you truly wish to relinquish these resentments, one suggestion is to write out in detail all your hurts and resentments. One woman who deeply resented her husband grinned broadly when I gave her this assignment and said, "Nancy, for the first time I'm going to enjoy my homework." Two weeks later she triumphantly presented me with an entire notebook she had filled just for the occasion! To her utter amazement, I instructed her to burn her notebook of resentment. While she watched the notebook go up in smoke, I instructed her to claim the promise found in Ephesians 4:31, 32—"Let all bitterness, and wrath, and anger, and clamour, and evil speaking, be put away from you, with all malice: and be ye kind one to another, tenderhearted, forgiving one another, even as God for Christ's sake hath forgiven you."

When she returned a week later, the transformation was dramatic. Her previously hard look had dramatically softened.

An aura of gentleness and youth clung to her. She now found many things about her husband that she appreciated and respected. It happened for her; it can happen for you. The desire for revenge keeps the past alive. Let someone else hate, hurt, and become bitter. You will be too smart to allow such poison to kill you. A new life in Jesus releases the pain of the past forever.

3. Reprogram your mind. If you are a single parent for whatever reason, stop thinking of yourself and defining yourself as a single parent. Define yourself once again as a "family," and refer to your family frequently as "our family," especially in the presence of your children. You haven't stopped being a family just because a member has departed. Think of your family in loving terms, as a closely knit unit, never as a crumbling heap about to disintegrate. Your new attitude will help the children too. Refrain from thinking of yourself as a loser, someone who no longer belongs, someone to be pitied. Stop longing for the family that could have been. Instead, accept the reality of what you have now. Determine to make the very best of your present circumstances.

4. Select a motto to provide encouragement. Such a motto might be "I can do all things through Christ which strengtheneth me" (Philippians 4:13). Print your motto on a small card, and place it in a prominent spot at home or the office—on a mirror, on the refrigerator, on a window, on the dashboard of your car, on your desk—anyplace where you will see it frequently.

5. Work to change one behavior or attitude at a time. Anytime someone attempts to change a situation or a behavior, the tendency is to go in all directions at once, which usually creates more problems than it solves. It is much more effective to work on one area at a time. So choose a problem for which you can immediately experience a quick, simple success. The success you experience in changing the first behavior will provide impetus to tackle a more difficult behavior change in a week or two.

6. Don't expect to change overnight. It may have taken you years to get where you are now, and it may take time to get where you want to be. Behavior-modification experts tell us it takes twenty-one to forty-five days to change a habit. Therefore, if the attitude or habit you are trying to change has been with you for a while, hang in there! Mark Twain astutely remarked: "Habit is habit, and not to be flung out of the window by any man, but coaxed downstairs a step at a time." Your behavior, through God's power, can be changed! But it takes consistent effort.

7. *Look for signs of improvement.* From time to time you will likely fail in your new program. Old behaviors sometimes stick closer than a brother. But rather than giving up your program because of a failure or two, reassess your progress. Where were you with this behavior when you began, and how far have you come? If you are failing fewer times this week than last, you are making progress! You (and God) are changing your behavior.

8. *Picture yourself, in advance, skillfully handling a problem situation.* Visual imaging, as it is called, is an important, practical, and powerful psychological tool. Anyone willing to concentrate can practice it. In advance of a problem situation, rehearse in your mind what strategy and action you will follow, then plot a better plan. The more specific you can be in your thinking, the more effectively you can predetermine the best course of action to follow. Picture yourself encountering the situation, calmly assessing the cause, and in controlled manner choosing the wisest plan of action to follow. Visualize your reaction, your words, your facial expressions, your tone of voice. This is the kind of dynamic imaging that can reap great and unexpected rewards for you.

9. *Watch for a chain-reaction effect.* It is a fact that if one person in a family starts functioning better, sooner or later (sometimes after a few storms) others in the family will do the same also. The positive emotional climate of the home will become contagious. And when families change, we know there

will be a reverberation in the neighborhood, in the church, and in the entire nation.

You will make mistakes from time to time in your new plan, but accept that fact and continue to move forward. When you get so discouraged that you might wish to throw in the towel, focus on what you have accomplished since the beginning of your program. Forget about your failures. Remember, when you are getting kicked from behind, it means you are in front!

You may be carrying a load of guilt over past mistakes. Don't blame yourself for what has happened. Don't let yesterday use up too much of today. The past is past. You did the best you knew how with the knowledge you had at the time. To whip yourself mercilessly with endless guilt or to blame others for what has happened will not solve anything, but it will hinder your growth process.

Whatever your mistakes in this area, God will accept you where you are and set you free from the load you are carrying. God always deals with us as we are today, now, not yesterday or ten years ago. Today you have a fresh opportunity to approach Him and go forward in faith. Paul talks about "forgetting what lies behind and reaching forward to what lies ahead" (Philippians 3:13, N.A.S.B.). Focus your eyes, your heart, and your mind on Him. Allow Him to work in your life today.

An item in a church bulletin read: "Spiritual growth class postponed until September." Spiritual growth is not something that can be put off. Either we are progressing or regressing. Remember, the world is round, and the place that seems like the end may be only the beginning. Venture forth with a new determination to do all you can to build a family with what you have and in keeping with God's plan. No one will ever be perfect here, but if you follow the God-given blueprint for happiness, you will discover wonderful happiness, and you can set a right example to the world.

Through Christ you can have a hope for the future that goes beyond the broken dreams, promises, and hurt you may have experienced from other people. Through God you can obtain a vision of your potential if you can only gain the courage to face the problem—to begin to risk, to start over again. Remodeling may require growing pains, but look to the Master Architect for a finished product. From this day forward you and He together can build a family happiness that can face the storms of life triumphantly!

Chapter 5

Courtship

—Preparing Models for the Future

When a girl says No to a proposal she expects to be held for further questioning.

The young couple seated in the counselor's office had not yet celebrated their first wedding anniversary, and already they found themselves locked in frequent battles. Just eight months earlier 19-year-old Sharon had made a stunning bride. Now, she fought back the tears in vain. "Marriage is so different from what I thought it would be," she sobbed.

Roger, her husband, was equally disturbed and resentful. "Sharon began to change right after the wedding," he said with evident bewilderment. "Before marriage we agreed on everything and could talk about anything. But that came to a rapid halt the minute we got back from our honeymoon. I've tried to bring up our problems for discussion, but she fights all my suggestions, cries a lot, and refuses to talk about changes that need to be made. Our relationship isn't at all what I had hoped it might be. Where do we go from here?"

They decided that they were incompatible, so they sought professional help. Truth is, any couple might be incompatible if they don't know what they are doing. It happens far too often with young people today, because they are not being prepared for dating, courtship, or marriage. What little preparation they do get will never suffice. So young people do the best they can, stumbling along—hoping, dreaming, and praying that somehow everything will turn out all right.

But this isn't good enough, and it wasn't good enough for Roger and Sharon. They were not incompatible. They were ignorant! They had proceeded toward marriage with romantic notions about what it takes to live together as husband and wife. All the while, they made no serious attempt to find out what it would take on their part to achieve a compleat marriage.

Why do so many marriages fail today? There are many reasons, but an important reason is a lack of preparation. Every couple needs to see successful marriage as a cherished goal—difficult to attain, but not unattainable. Couples who drift into marriage, thinking that it will provide their lifelong quest for lasting bliss, are being unrealistic. Those who think that love will take care of everything that stands in the way are courting a dangerous philosophy.

Someone has noted that we send children to school for ten to fifteen years so they can learn a vocation. Yet we teach them practically nothing about marriage, which is ultimately more important than any profession.

In order to turn the tide of divorce sweeping this crumbling world in which we live, I recommend that *no one should enter marriage without a series of effective studies on marriage and the interpersonal relationships that lead to marriage.* Such an approach might not entirely correct the problem, but it would certainly be a good start. Let's take a close look at how couples can get the most from the dating and courtship period of life.

The Most Popular Game on Earth—The Dating Game!

He calls to ask for a date. She quivers a shaky "OK," then calls twenty of her friends to let them know he has finally asked her out. She spends hours on her physical appearance so she looks as much like the TV commercials as possible. He saves his money so he has a few extra bucks to impress her. The night of "the big date" arrives, and he drives up. She keeps him waiting a few minutes—not long enough so that he gets angry, but just long enough so he becomes curious. She floats down the stairs. He opens the door. They're off—and the dating game begins. . . .

Dating poses one of the greatest mountains that face young adults today. Frequently young adults experience frustration, discouragement, and depression over this important aspect of their lives. Some feel guilt-ridden because of sexual involvements. Others suffer depression because they have no one to date or because they care for someone who fails to return their affection. Meanwhile, television and radio programs, movies, billboards, magazines, novels, and a myriad of other sources provide an almost constant diet of misinformation about love, sex, and marriage.

Dating is a special kind of friendship between two persons of the opposite sex. Ideally, it progresses through six stages.

The first stage is friendship. Yes, dating springs from a friendship, and the better a young person is at developing good friendships, the more successful he or she will be at this stage of dating. Good dating relationships should grow out of good friendships.

In casual dating, the second stage, a couple date for the pleasure of having a member of the opposite sex with whom to share enjoyable activities. Casual dating usually involves relationships with a number of individuals. The degree of emotional commitment to each other at this stage is very low or even nonexistent.

The third stage, special dating, includes such activities as annual banquets, fancy affairs, and special events that require an escort. This stage involves a certain amount of emotional commitment, but it is usually on the low side unless the couple are already committed to each other.

The fourth stage, commonly known as going steady, means that the couple have committed themselves to date only each other. The depth of emotional commitment will vary with the couple. Some take steady dating seriously and form long-lasting relationships. Others use it as a means of "social security." Most couples consider themselves "in love" at this stage.

A fifth, and relatively newly recognized stage, engaged-to-be-engaged, applies to the period between going steady and becoming officially engaged. The couple talk in terms of a permanent relationship and make *tentative* plans toward marriage. Their understanding is private and personal, and not final or binding. They make no formal announcement, nor are wedding plans in progress. The couple talk in terms of "someday when we get married . . ."

The sixth, and final, stage before marriage is the formal engagement. Here the couple publicly announce their intention to marry, plan the wedding, and seriously pursue the exploration of each other's personality. The male usually presents to his bride-to-be a symbol of some kind that binds their commitment to one another.

Unfortunately, too often couples get things backward. They jump to the going steady or engaged-to-be-engaged stage without ever becoming friends first! They are so eager to fall in love that they attempt to skip the preliminaries. But love and all the "romantic stuff" should follow a solid friendship. Frequently I talk with married couples about becoming "best friends" with their mates, but such an idea sounds bizarre to many people. Such couples have fallen into love so rapidly they never really learned if they "liked" one another first. Yet quality feelings of friendship can go a long way in a marriage relationship.

Charlotte and Charlie met at a singles' retreat. Both were sincere Christians who had been praying earnestly that God would send along a mate. It was a clearcut case of love at first sight for both of them. Six weeks later they were married, and six months later they sought our advice because of their disastrous relationship. In a letter to me later, Charlie wrote: "I thought that because we were both committed Christians, we would have a great marriage.'' Then he added bitterly, ''The fact that we are Christians has kept us from killing each other, but that doesn't guarantee a happy marriage!''

Where did this couple make their mistake? In attempting to move from stage 1 to stage 6 of the dating game in six weeks! It simply can't be done. I personally recommend that every couple date for two years prior to their engagement. And this rule of thumb is applicable even for (especially for) those who have been previously married. I may sound hard-nosed, but some of the biggest fiascoes I've witnessed involve previously married individuals who think they are ''experienced'' and therefore can skip all ''the kid stuff.'' No one, regardless of age or experience, can beat the test of time. It takes a full year of dating someone on a regular basis for all the ''masks'' to begin slipping—and longer to see the real person.

Dating at its best should allow for personality development, help individuals to understand the opposite sex, fill the need for human love, supply opportunities for fun and recreation, assist in the selection of a marriage partner, and be instrumental in helping persons to develop spiritually. At its best, dating provides a workshop in which one can develop the skills needed to achieve a positive intimate relationship in marriage. At its worst, dating exploits and uses others as a means to an end.

It takes awhile during the dating game to be able to judge ''datability.'' In one revealing study 90 percent of the students polled felt they were ''good'' dates. However, when the same males and females rated each other, they were quite critical of each other's dating abilities! A lack of respect and courtesy, along with rudeness and inconsiderate behavior; heavy drinking, swearing, drugs, and smoking; failure to plan for the date, with attempts to get the female to decide; aggressive attempts to neck, especially on first dates; and too much bragging and self-conceit turned off the young ladies.

Males dislike females who are conceited, self-centered,

artificial, and difficult to please; who act like "gold diggers"; who place too much emphasis on "rating" in choice of dates; who insist on being asked too far in advance for dates; and who are habitually late for dates. One male added to this list: "Women who brag about all the other guys they have dated."

When the researcher asked the students what qualities and values were the most important in both casual and serious dating, the following seven traits appeared according to rank: (1) physical and mental fitness, (2) dependability, (3) pride in personal appearance and manner, (4) clean speech and action, (5) pleasant disposition and sense of humor, (6) consideration and thoughtfulness, and (7) acting one's age and not being childish.

Success in dating depends largely upon personality, behavior, and appearance. But these things are determined to a great degree by one's self-concept. All the do's and don'ts for a great dating future aren't helpful if a person cherishes negative feelings about self. Who wants to be around someone who is always running himself or others down, or feeling sorry for himself, or lacking confidence in his ability to do things?

Basically there are two kinds of dates (and I don't mean good ones and bad ones!)—spectator and participation dates.

Spectator dates include movies, concerts, sporting events, watching TV, or listening to records. Spectator dates are common, popular, and fun. They are particularly popular on first dates because they reduce the stress involved in keeping up your end of a conversation with someone you do not as yet know well. Furthermore, everyone can do it—sit and watch, that is.

On the other hand, spectator events are often expensive, and they allow less time to develop a friendship through conversation, which defeats one of the main purposes in dating—getting to know each other better. Besides, we already do too much sitting and watching. Spectating does very little to nurture feelings of self-worth, requires little creativity, and will likely ensure that you tire of each other more quickly than in other kinds of activity.

Participation dates include playing games; canoeing; sailing; visiting museums, art galleries, and zoos; and planning and cooking a meal together. Participation dates allow outlets for creative abilities and afford fewer opportunities for sexual temptations. This type of date reaffirms feelings of worth and helps develop skills and abilities, as well as providing insights about your date. Usually participation dates cost less and allow both partners to get to know each other better than do spectator dates. Since participation dates offer far more advantages, they should make up a larger portion of the dating experience than spectator dating.

The dating years are precious years and should be used to full advantage. They provide a time for developing honorable values, worthwhile goals, and excellent standards of behavior. Young people should get involved, meet new people, and date a lot. They shortchange themselves when they limit their opportunities to one person during the early years. Everyone who comes in contact with your life will leave a part of himself or herself with you. You can learn lessons even from a complete bore, braggart, or a gossip—lessons like tolerance. So give yourself a real basis for comparison. Don't be like the fly in the bottle of vinegar who thinks it is the sweetest place in the world because it is the only place he has ever been!

Breaking Up Is Hard to Do

The dating game usually forms a cycle—dating around, going steady, breaking up; dating around, going steady, breaking up; and so forth. With the exception of the person you eventually marry, you will break up or drift away from every person you date. But how the situation is handled when break-up time comes is crucial.

Occasions arise when it is healthier to break off a relationship than to keep it going. Some couples become so wrapped up in each other that they fail to see the danger signals that could make shipwreck of their future. Danger signals include extreme arguing and fighting, extreme physical involvement, conflicting goals and values, physical or mental abuse, withdrawal from friends and activities, and a poor combination of personalities, along with others not mentioned.

Anyone who has doubts about a decision to call it quits should seek advice from a trusted and respected friend. Many couples break up during the heat of an argument and later wish they hadn't. The objective opinion of someone not emotionally involved in the situation often proves helpful.

Pray about it, asking the Lord to make it clear that you have chosen the right course of action. *If possible,* give the other person a warning. An abrupt break can have the same kind of impact as a sudden death. During the breaking-up process, spare the other person's feelings of worth. (It is a major loss to have someone whom you love reject you.) Then end the relationship as soon as you have decided, rather than leading the other person on. Try to emphasize all the good times you have had, what the other has contributed to your friendship, as well as your appreciation for his or her finer qualities. Sort out why things went wrong and the part you played in it.

Be truthful about your reasons for breaking up, even though it may hurt the other person. It is better to be told why than to continue wondering what you said or did to cause it. After the breakup, make sure you avoid broadcasting any personal information about your relationship.

How do you cope when someone you care about deeply indicates that he or she no longer wants a romantic relationship with you? Handle it with class. It's up to you. You can salvage your self-esteem or else create an ugly, messy scene that can leave lasting scars.

Feel free to talk it over. You may not understand why it is over, but bow out gracefully, assuring the other person that you want to be friends. You may ask why if your partner does not tell you. But when all has been said and done, accept the situation as it is and use it to your advantage rather than detriment. Instead of looking and acting like your world has fallen apart, carry your self-respect away with you.

If you feel like crying about it, go ahead—and this advice goes for males as well as females. The longer you have gone together and the more close the relationship, the deeper your grief will be. Also, give yourself a chance to heal before immediately seeking another relationship. Time is a wonderful healer, although some people take longer to recuperate than others. After you have sorted out your responsibility for what happened, talk it over with a friend and then get on with life. You might be tempted to bask in your own misery, but put the past behind you and keep it there.

One more thing. Pray about it. God knows and cares about what has happened to you. Tell Him how you hurt, and ask Him to help you heal. Claim the promise that "all things work together for good to them that love God" (Romans 8:28). He has a purpose in allowing hurt to touch our lives. It may seem as though the pain will never go away, but when you least expect it, suddenly you'll realize that you have put yourself back together again.

How to Tell if You Are Really in Love

"Mom, I'm really in love!" sighed our 19-year-old-son, Rodney, dramatically as he staged mock weakness of knees and staggered around before me. Although he said it in a lighthearted manner, he was dead serious. He had found the girl of his dreams. She not only looked good but also had an outgoing personality and was creative and gifted. After checking her out, Harry and I had to admit that she was a perfect complement for Rodney. Yet only nine months later this encounter in "real love" between two great young people was over. In spite of the intensity of their first impressions, their "love" went the way of so many other romances—downhill.

According to psychological studies, most people will have

somewhere between seven and ten romances in a lifetime. Only one or two of these romances will be genuine love. You may already have experienced a portion of your allotment. But the big question is "How can I tell for sure when I am really in love or when I am infatuated?"

Although volumes have been devoted to the subject of love, almost no studies have been conducted to determine the components, effects, or results of infatuation. This is unfortunate because infatuation causes no end of heartache for those caught in its trap of deception.

Love and infatuation do have one thing in common—strong feelings of affection for a member of the opposite sex, which complicates the matter of sorting out the differences. Many of the symptoms overlap one another. The most passionate and blind infatuation may contain a portion of genuine love. And genuine love may include a certain amount of infatuation. *The differences between love and infatuation, then, are often found in degree rather than in definition.*

Here are twelve factors to help you discern the difference between love and infatuation. For a full description of each of these items please read my book *The Compleat Courtship*, chapter 5.

1. Love develops slowly; infatuation rapidly.
2. Love ends slowly; infatuation ends rapidly.
3. Love centers on one person only; infatuation may involve several persons.
4. Love motivates positive behavior; infatuation has a destructive effect.
5. Love recognizes the importance of compatibility; infatuation disregards it.
6. Love recognizes faults; infatuation ignores them.
7. Love survives separation; infatuation cannot.
8. Love controls physical contact; infatuation exploits it.
9. Love is selfless; infatuation is selfish.
10. Love brings the approval of family and friends;

infatuation brings disapproval.

    11.   Love produces security; infatuation produces insecurity.

    12.   Love recognizes realities; infatuation ignores them.

If you have analyzed your situation as carefully as you can but still can't decide whether or not you have found true love, if the more you try to figure it out the more confused you get, allow a little more time to pass. Time will give you experience and perspective. It will offer you more contact with your friend. It will provide more opportunities for you to find out what you need to know in order to make the final decision. After all is said and done, you have found genuine love when your mutual relationship fosters individual growth for both of you and increases the depth of your love for each other from this day forward.

Touchy Situations

Next to dating, petting seems to be the most popular sport. In a study I personally conducted of young people ages 16 to 25, I learned that a whopping 79 percent had engaged in petting activities to one degree or another.

Although petting is widespread, the rules vary tremendously. Young people tend to wing it, making up their own rules as they go. Petting includes a wide range of body-exploring activities, and every group of young people seems to have its own definition of what constitutes light and heavy petting.

Whatever its definition, petting is an activity that says something important. It goes a step beyond hugging and kissing but not as far as intercourse. When a couple engage in petting, they feel they are saying, "I love you and care about you. Someday our relationship may blossom into something more, but right now this is where things are."

Let's get one thing straight. Petting is not dirty. It will not give you a disease or make hair grow on your palms or curl your toes. Inside the bonds of marriage petting is a beautiful experience and is called foreplay, which leads to sexual intercourse. What, then, is the difference between petting and foreplay? Petting is the exploration of each other's body by two persons who do not intend for intercourse to occur. And that's the trouble with petting. It doesn't stand alone. It is designed to move on to something else. By itself, outside of marriage, it is generally more frustrating than satisfying.

Petting should not be viewed as an end in itself. It is a mistake to think of petting as only an adventure in the cool and calculated exploration of another person's body. Petting involves emotions and passions that all too quickly send inner controls into oblivion. Furthermore, petting is progressive. Next time you will want to go a step farther in order to get the same thrills you enjoyed last time.

Another interesting thing about petting is that it affects guys differently from the way it does girls. But since members of both sexes wear many masks, they often do not understand what the other is feeling. Society rears boys to be strong, tough, forceful, aggressive, and capable of functioning in many manly ways. Being capable sexually is one of the most important tests of masculinity.

Few females realize the many ways a male is stimulated sexually. He is more sex-driven than the female, and this holds true for him throughout life. Men are more visually oriented than women and have a stronger desire to prove their manhood than women do to prove their femininity. Peer pressure motivates many males to improve their position with the crowd, to accept a dare, and to make out or whatever with a girl. Some devious males play at love as though it were a contest and therefore exploit women. Others use sex as a form of rebellion, to show superiority, or as a thrilling adventure.

Males who do not really understand the female nature often assume that a woman is as eager to make out as they are. Actually, females respond much more slowly. It isn't that a woman cannot respond; it's just that she takes longer. He responds more to physical factors, whereas she responds to emotional ones. So here we have a guy and a girl involved in petting. He's enjoying every minute of it and secretly hopes she'll get carried away and give him what he really wants. She probably isn't as aroused as he is. What she's enjoying is not the physical thrills as much as the feeling of being "loved."

When a woman engages in petting activities, she usually does so for reasons different from the man's. Women pet in order to get love, to achieve popularity, to work out feelings of rebellion (particularly against parents), and to see how far they can go with a fellow. Someone has described a smart girl as one who can hold a man at arm's length without losing her grip on him.

When we conduct a Compleat Courtship Seminar, one of the most frequently asked questions is "How far is too far?" Aren't people interesting? They always want to know how far they can go and still stay within the limits of propriety. Other than warnings against intercourse outside of marriage, the Bible never explains whether petting is right or wrong. But Biblical guidelines governing relationships with the opposite sex should enable us to make some judgments concerning our behavior.

1. The Bible condemns sexual intercourse for unmarried people. Check John 8:41; Acts 15:20-29; Romans 1:29; 1 Corinthians 6:13, 18; 2 Corinthians 12:21; Ephesians 5:3. Thirty-seven times in the Bible God excludes premarital sex from His plan for men and women. Therefore, any petting activities that lead to sexual intercourse will be "too far."

2. You have gone too far if you unduly arouse sexual desires. Almost all fellows have problems after prolonged kissing, whether *she* realizes it or not. If the tension becomes so strong that passion dictates action, then you're in trouble.

3. If your conscience bothers you, you have gone too far. One of the functions of the Holy Spirit is to convict us of sin through our conscience. If your conscience tells you that something you are doing is wrong and you do it anyway, then it becomes a sin. (See Romans 14:23; 1 John 3:21.)

4. *You have gone too far when nudity is involved.* In several places the Old Testament associates nakedness with illicit sexual conduct. To "uncover another's nakedness" means to have intercourse, since there is total intimacy when you remove your clothing. When an unmarried couple remove their clothing or if they caress under the clothing, they have gone too far.

5. *You have gone too far if it hurts your relationship.* Petting can hurt your relationship by keeping you from developing the techniques necessary for getting and staying in touch with each other. Some couples have indulged so heavily in physical intimacies prior to marriage that they never could develop meaningful verbal communication. When petting gets going, verbal communication shuts down.

Long before you fondle the erotic areas of another person's body, your total life experience has determined how far you will go. How do you feel about yourself? What takes first place in your life? Whom or what do you idolize? What do you expect from yourself in life? What are your values? What goals have you set for your life? In short, the sum total of your character begins to emerge now. You have started to write your life story. Will the script glorify God?

Close Encounters of a Dangerous Kind

Did you know that:

* One of every two Americans between 15 and 19 years of age is sexually active, but only one in every five uses some method of contraception or birth control?
* 2,740 teenagers get pregnant every day?
* 1,282 illegitimate babies are born every day?
* 3,231 women have abortions every day?
* 3,000 persons become infected with a sexually transmitted disease every day—60 percent of them in their teens?

A recent television program on teenage sexuality reported that there are more sex acts, more pregnancies, more abortions, and fewer marriages among sexually active couples today than ever before in history. More and more of today's young people question traditional morality. They judge premarital sex not in terms of whether it is right or wrong but whether it is a genuine expression of love that they should use in their relationship. No longer do young people ask, ''Is it right or wrong?'' but ''Is it right for us in our relationship?''

Premarital sex has both plus and minus aspects to it. In my book *The Compleat Courtship,* a list is included of the advantages of premarital sex (yes, there are some!) and the disadvantages. Here I'll give only two advantages.

1. The more premarital sexual experience women have prior to marriage, the more likely they are to experience a full orgasm during intercourse in the first year of marriage. But, in spite of their ability to reach orgasm, far more of the wives in these studies had sex difficulties during the early days of marriage, and significant numbers reported long-term difficulties.

2. Premarital sex can be fun. Sex is one of the most pleasurable experiences given by God for men and women to enjoy. His infinite mind originated the idea of sex—the union between male and female that brings more physical pleasure than any other activity. Whether intercourse fulfills a desire to have children, satisfies the sex drive, reassures each other of love, or relaxes the nervous system, it all adds up to providing the most exciting physical experience known to humans. God created sex for our pleasure, and He wants us to delight in it. Sex is an enjoyable experience whether the couple engage in it prior to marriage or after.

From my list of twenty disadvantages to premarital sex, I'll mention only three here.

1. Premarital sex tends to break up couples. Studies show that couples (even engaged couples) who engage in sex before marriage are more likely to break up than those who do not. Why? One reason is that the male's need for marriage lessens when his sex needs are being satisfied outside marriage. Once the "ultimate" has been done, it leaves little curiosity to probe the mystery beyond. When a sexually active couple break up, it is far more painful than if they had never entered a sexual liaison.

2. *Premarital sex increases the risk of cervical cancer among young women who engage in sex with multiple partners.* About the time menstruation begins, the entire endocrine system is being stabilized and the finishing touches are completing the intricate development of the uterus, fallopian tubes, and ovaries. The cervix is extremely vulnerable during this time. If it is exposed to semen, whether from one or multiple partners, it can set the stage for carcinoma (cancer) of the cervix later on in life. Research shows that the younger a girl becomes sexually active, the more partners she has, and the more frequent the sexual exposure during those years, the higher her chances are of contracting cervical cancer during ages 40 to 45.

3. *Those who have premarital sex are less happy in marriage and more prone to divorce.* The more premarital sex a couple has, the less likely they will have a happy married life. Their past often rises to haunt them. It also increases the likelihood of extramarital sex. Studies relating premarital sex to extramarital coitus show that those who have had premarital experience are twice as likely to have extramarital affairs as those who are virgins at marriage.

Do you want to take these kinds of chances with your future?

Living together enjoys an unparalleled popularity today. The latest census figures reveal that in the past ten years the number of unmarried couples living together has jumped astronomically. Rarely have investigators discovered such a rapid change in any type of social behavior.

Perhaps you have considered living with someone without benefit of marriage. You may have toyed with the idea in order to avoid the tragedy of divorce. If two persons love each other, why can't they just live together without being bound by the

Bible or guilt? Who needs a wedding, anyway? What difference does a piece of paper make?

First of all, a wedding means something to society, the state, and the church. It publicly declares that a new family has been established. Second, the wedding is a safeguard for moral standards. It provides a legitimate name for children and provides right to each other's property according to the laws of the community. Third, it protects individuals from abuse and exploitation, preventing such things as bigamy, fraud, the use of force, and the marriage of under-age children or seriously incompetent persons. It also guards the legality of the wedding agreement.

Furthermore, studies indicate that a sexual relationship may hold a couple together for three to five years, but no longer. Therefore, a couple who live together would have to pass the three- to five-year mark in order to find out if they had really found genuine love.

What should you do if you have already gone too far? First of all, you do not need to feel unclean or subhuman. And you are not obligated to marry a person just because you have had intercourse, even if pregnancy has resulted. To marry just to give a baby a name is one of the least valid reasons for marriage. The remedy will not be easy, but here are some suggestions.

1. Acknowledge your mistake. To rationalize that you "accidentally" went all the way is not facing the truth. When both parties freely and willfully seek a place of privacy where they can spend time alone together, and they progress from light to heavy petting, intercourse is no accident. The sooner a couple admit it is a *choice,* the sooner they will be able to handle the problem and cope with the guilt.

2. Ask God for forgiveness. Confession is good for the soul, and we serve a God who will totally and completely forgive our sins when we truly repent. He will help us through our mistakes so we can become stronger, finer, and more complete persons.

3. If you wish to test whether the relationship is genuine love or infatuation, there is one way to find out. Refuse to see each other for a long period of time, preferably several months. You may write or phone each other, but you must avoid any opportunities to be alone together. A couple who attempt to sidestep this aspect will only deceive themselves.

Despite what's been said so far, let's say that you plan to take advantage of the next situation that presents itself (and you know in your heart whether or not you will). If this is your intention, and you insist on indulging in sex outside of marriage, please protect yourselves against sexually transmitted disease and unwanted pregnancy. This means that *both of you should use some form of contraception.* When you take the time for double protection, it gives you time to think. I know it isn't very romantic, but then neither is unmarried parenthood or a sexually transmitted disease.

Are You Fit to Be Tied?

A Peanuts cartoon shows Charlie Brown talking with Lucy. Charlie says, ''I'd like to be able to feel that I'm needed.'' Lucy replies, ''Don't forget, Charlie Brown, that people who are really needed are asked to do a lot of different things.'' He thinks it over, then quips, ''I'd like to feel needed and yet not have to do anything.'' Such immaturity proves that Charlie Brown is not ready for marriage.

Marriage offers the most rewards when the relationship is a *mutual* meeting of personality needs. Maturity includes understanding the nature of love and the various levels and types of love you have experienced to the present. It also includes developing your religious concepts, values, and goals and living in accordance with what you believe to be right and good. A mature person will accurately evaluate himself or herself and will be working to improve weaknesses when possible and build on strengths. To test your fitness for marriage means to take inventory of your family background, the contribution it has made to making you what and who you are, and what you will bring to marriage from your background.

Maturity calls for meeting problems constructively, and not allowing the frustrations of life to throw you into fits of confusion, discouragement, or disorganization. You will have learned about interpersonal relationships that prompt behavior in yourself and others. You will have achieved a degree of independent thinking which facilitates the ability to think for yourself. You will have outgrown the inclination to blame others for your weaknesses and can accept responsibility for your own mistakes. You will have developed positive and wholesome attitudes about sex.

Naturally, the maturity that is expected of you is also expected of your partner. But since none of us ever reaches the same level of maturity in the same area at the same time, it is difficult to judge whether someone else is mature. Danger signals do not always show up early in a relationship. Therefore, I always recommend relatively long periods of courtship prior to engagement. The people who rush toward marriage without recognizing any danger signals often are the least prepared for it.

Every normal person seaches for his or her "one and only." But searching for that one person is a lost cause. A well-adjusted person can marry any one of several persons and be happy. On the other hand, it is highly unlikely that an immature person could be happy married to anyone. Marriage does not make an immature person mature or happy, but happy and mature people do make successful marriages.

Although the number of persons with whom you could successfully mate is great, this does not mean that you could make a go of marriage with just anyone. You must still choose wisely. The example parents have provided during the early years and the attitudes and training they have passed along to their children are the most important contributions parents can make to the future marital happiness of their children. That's why happiness runs in families—as does trouble, unhappiness, and divorce. If you were brought up in a family of constant bickering, you will probably carry the same behavior into your own relationships. If you were reared in a family that showed superior happiness through loving words, kind deeds, and deep affection, you will likely experience this.

But suppose you didn't have a happy home. What then? If you are willing to study and prepare yourself for marriage, you can overcome the handicaps in your background and break the cycle of marital unhappiness from this day forward. No one is bound by his background unless he chooses to be. Choose happiness, reap happiness! Choose success, reap success!

What is the ideal age for marrying? All studies to date conclude that early marriages are not as stable as those of more mature persons. Minimum age 22 for women and 24 for men seems to ensure a measure of success. Grooms under 24 are usually unstable, and the percentage of unsuccessful marriages when the groom is 19 or younger is very high. Couples who are 25 years of age or older have a better than 70 percent chance of success. And, according to psychologist Dr. Joyce Brothers, the happiest couples marry after age 28.

Religion plays an important part in marriage, and years of research have indicated that those who belong to no religious group have a greater marriage risk than those who do. In marriages where one person is religious and the other not, the divorce and delinquency rates among their children are generally twice as high as in marriages where both partners share the same faith. A couple's involvement in spiritual activities contributes to a successful relationship both during engagement and marriage. And couples who attend religious services regularly after marriage report a high degree of marital satisfaction. Without a doubt, religion makes a significant contribution to the success of marriage.

All research shows that partners in mixed-faith marriages usually experience trouble and seek separations sooner than do same-faith marriages. Conflict in mixed-faith marriages centers on four fundamental issues: (1) over what religion the children will follow, (2) over church attendance, (3) over interference by in-laws in religious matters, and (4) over size of family and/or spacing of children. One reason the divorce rate is higher in mixed-faith marriages may be that during courtship a couple minimizes the difficulties likely to be encountered and consequently large reality conflicts can develop after the honeymoon glow has died down.

Religion *is* an asset to marriage. The committed religious person has a greater chance for marital happiness when married to an individual of like interests. The virtues extolled in the Bible—meekness, kindness, consideration for others, helpful-ness, selflessness—help to make a well-adjusted personality. Those who have captured such values and have learned to apply them successfully in real-life situations generally make good prospects for marriage. I do not mean to imply that a nonreligious person cannot possess such characteristics, only that there is greater likelihood that a person will develop them than if he or she belongs to a group that teaches and practices such values.

Marriage to a divorced person is another serious matter to be considered. It is easy for a person who has never been married to think, ''His or her past has no bearing on our future together. That is over and done with. It was not his or her fault.'' But marriage to a divorced person is not the same as a marriage in which both partners are uniting for the first time.

A couple who had been attending our courtship seminar sought my advice regarding the possibility of marriage. She was 29, twice divorced, and the mother of two children (one from each previous marriage). Her friend was 31 and in the process of a lengthy divorce that had been in the courts for three years. He had three children. They had become acquainted three months earlier and had found themselves drawn together and compati-ble. They wanted to know what I thought about the advisability of marriage within five months. With a gentle smile I told them that they might be very well suited for each other, but I wouldn't even discuss the advisability of marriage with them until they had dated for another year. With a grin the man said, "I knew you were going to say that!"

Society looks upon second marriages in a different light. There is not the optimistic acceptance that usually accompanies a first marriage. There is the strong likelihood of family opposition. The family of the previously unmarried partner tends to view the marriage with mingled hope and fear, and the family of the divorced person cannot help making comparisons between the first and second choice of partners. If the previous marriage has produced children, additional factors must be considered.

If you are considering marriage to a divorced person, you need to be particularly alert in evaluating his or her personality and adjustability. Statistically speaking, a divorced person poses a greater marriage risk than the one who has not been married before, and the divorced woman is an even greater risk than the divorced man.

Many people can't wait to prove the test of time and hence rush into marriage. They fail to develop a better and higher kind of love relationship. But there is a blueprint for happiness. So from this day forward allow God to work in your behalf. Prove the test of time and allow two full years of regular dating. Remember, God always bestows the best on those who seek His help in choosing.

Chapter 6

Today's Family
—Beginning Heaven in Your Haven With a Canopy of Love

The best gift of all: The presence of a happy family all wrapped up in each other.

An American general once uttered a brief but profound observation about war: "The only way to win a war is to prevent it." Can his words also apply to the family? When family members declare war on each other, no one wins.

In some families it's difficult to spot trouble right away, but that doesn't mean the potential for trouble isn't there underneath the surface. A woman confided to me at a recent seminar, "Everyone thinks we're the ideal family. But it's all a lie. No one really knows what goes on in our home!" She was existing in a home barren of the satisfactions that family living should provide—sharing, friendship, closeness, and affection. On the surface everyone saw what appeared to be a stable family, but the very foundation was quaking.

As someone who is concerned about your fulfillment and your family, I invite you to take a closer look at the experience of family living the way God designed. He has provided all the pleasures known to mankind, and as the Creator of the family and the Author of joy, He wants every family to enjoy a life of satisfaction and happiness, not just a favored few.

Self-respect: A Family Affair

Every family member must develop a healthy self-respect. And since the origin of self-respect can be traced to the tender years of childhood, the development of this key attribute is a family affair. It is within the family that we first measure our worth, lovability, and capability. Therefore, the nurturing each family member gives and receives becomes priority one.

After the launching point of my career as a family life educator it did not take me long to realize that a lack of self-worth is the culprit in an overwhelming majority of troubled homes. Self-worth is the pivotal point that determines what happens inside people and between people—it's the mental picture of worth locked in the mind at all times.

Family living is relatively easy with the person whose Christ-centered self-esteem is high. From the person who has a positive reflection of self, flow love, compassion, responsibility, and cooperation. Such people have confidence in their own abilities. Since they appreciate their own worth, they are free to appreciate the worth of others and accept each family member as he or she is. People with healthy self-respect are free to make decisions as need be, but they are so secure that they can readily ask for help when necessary, thus validating the worth of other family members in the process.

Other people, however, spend the majority of their lives looking in negative mirrors. I frequently ask persons who seek me out for personal guidance regarding family problems to evaluate their worth on a scale of one to ten, with ten being high self-worth. One, two, or three are common numbers given. One woman with a very troubled background buried her face in her hands and sobbed, "I hate myself, I hate myself, I hate myself!" I knew we could make little progress with her problems until she discarded her negative mirror.

In my book *The Compleat Parent* I devote an entire chapter

to instructing parents how to help their child develop positive feelings of worth. It is an important task, but it is also possible to get so involved in building a child's self-esteem that the parents forget to do something for their own!

If positive affirmations are good for little people, they must also be good for family leaders! Parents sometimes get cross and depressed. They quarrel with each other and even forget what they quarreled about. Their energy and patience reach the bottom of the barrel. The demands of family life are sometimes so great that the emotional barometer flashes an unwelcome "STRESS, STRESS, STRESS!" signal. Someone must keep parents' needs met and their mirror positive, or they will not have the energy or ability to fulfill their child's needs.

Husbands and wives, parents and children, need to experiment with different ways of affirming one another. Any extended members of the household should also be part of this program. Sometimes people feel awkward when they first begin affirming one another and stop trying. But if you take the time to reevaluate how you felt before you began the reaffirmation program, you'll probably notice that you now have more energy and are less quarrelsome than when you weren't using this positive method of affirming one another.

How can you begin? It might work like this: At breakfast Mother says to her child in front of Dad, "Chuck, you did a super job of picking up your room and making your bed. I'm proud of the fine way you're accepting responsibility." A hug then adds the ribbon to the package.

In another instance husband might say to wife, "I enjoy being with you. I'd rather be with you than anyone else I know." And he seals those sentiments with a lingering kiss. Who can know, looking into life's future of companionship together, just how much admiration and respect she will possess for him as a direct result of those tender seeds sown in her heart by her faithful, romantic, loving husband?

Wife might say to husband, "Honey, you did a great job of

repairing the car. I'm sure you saved us a lot of money. I'm proud to be married to you.'' This, along with a pat on the back, would make his chest swell.

Such affirmations should be voiced three times a day at least, privately and publicly. Public affirmations subtly teach (without preaching) how each family member can reinforce the positive mirror of others. Children will begin to copy the behavior they see modeled by Mother and Father. Public affirmations can be followed by a multitude of private and personal affirmations. Whispering a warm, loving message, sitting close, holding hands, a wink, telephone calls, love notes, and intimate back rubs all say: ''I like you. You're special to me. I think you're great.''

Just today, as murmurings of an impending divorce among our circle of friends surfaced, Harry held me close and whispered, ''I'm so lucky to have you. We have so much going for us and so little apart. I thank God for you.'' The security of his arms about me reinforced my worth as an individual and as a marriage partner, along with enhancing the security of our relationship. Oh, for thousands of Harrys who would daily affirm their wives' worth through words of endearment and fond gestures of affection! I personally believe such behavior among partners would cut the present divorce rate in half.

We all need family and friends to build our positive mirrors. But our friends and family should not be totally responsible for filling our needs. We are responsible for taking care of some of our own needs so as not to put excess demands on others. It is especially important for single parents—those with unsupportive mates—and women to remember.

You can and should give affirmations to yourself. Write out some encouraging words on cards and put them in the window over the kitchen sink, on the bathroom mirror, on your desk, or on the dashboard of your car. Think good thoughts. Be good to yourself!

Did you realize that the more positive your self-concept, the more affirmation you will be able to store up and keep for a future low period? Another thing, the more positive your mirror, the easier it is for you to give others high-quality affirmations. When you see yourself in a negative light, you project to others your negative feelings. When your self-worth dips to such a low level, you also look and feel awful. Storing up a few affirmations for these inevitable low times will help you get over a few rough spots in your life.

One-on-One—It's a Two-way Street

Communication between and among family members is the second important part in the blueprint for family happiness. In the book *Peoplemaking* family therapist Dr. Virginia Satir states that in her practice just about everyone who is having serious problems coping with life—school problems, alcoholism, adultery, whatever—was communicating with others in destructive patterns. Most of these destructive patterns arise from low feelings of worth. The close connection between self-respect and communication now becomes evident.

Other problems that plague family life also spring spontaneously from ineffective communication patterns. Quarrels, arguments, misunderstandings, disappointed expectations, and a whole gamut of difficulties find their genesis in a lack of effective communication. Many families get caught in such a web of poor habits of communication, which have gone on for so many years, that disentanglement appears nearly impossible. So they give up. But the truth is that since their poor methods of communication have been learned, they can be unlearned and subsequently changed.

Most family members do not deliberately set out to hurt, annoy, anger, or frustrate one another. More frequently these troubles arise because something was not made clear, and what usually has not been made clear is feelings. Furthermore, many people are so out of touch with their feelings that they couldn't identify them, much less make them clear!

There is a method of communicating with others in a direct manner that you can learn and then use in the daily minutiae of life. It will put you in touch with yourself, your family, and your feelings. It will help you develop honesty and intimacy even when you are grappling with problems. Your words will match your feelings, actions, and tone of voice.

All of this can be accomplished through "I-statements." I-statements identify your actual feelings and report them openly, honestly, and kindly. And I-statements are particularly useful when someone else's behavior irritates you.

An effective I-statement would sound something like this: "I can't concentrate on paying these bills when there's so much ruckus going on in here. It's extremely difficult to concentrate, and I'm getting a headache." The kids will look up, startled. "We're sorry," they chant. "We forgot you were working. We'll turn down the TV and be more quiet."

Simply report your personal feelings without put-downs and *without telling others what to do*. We all get defensive about being given orders. Restrain the natural instinct to add a solution message or an order at the end of your I-statement. Instead, frame your I-statements in the following manner: "I feel _____ when you _____ because _____."

This simple technique can do more to clean up irritating misunderstandings, hurt feelings, and unclear messages than any other single method. And it brings results. People are surprised to learn how the other person really feels. Often they say, "Why didn't you say something before?" We tend to underestimate the willingness of others to be more considerate once they know they are doing something that irritates us.

Children will also learn from I-statements direct methods of communicating their feelings. Rather than suppressing, blaming, and withdrawing, they will learn to express their feelings in an open, honest, yet kind manner.

Opening the Gates to the Two-way Street

How can you improve your communication from this moment on?

1. Choose the right time. Your subject may be well chosen, but your timing may be off. Select a time when the other person can respond pleasantly.

2. Develop a pleasant tone of voice. It isn't always *what* you say, but *how* you say it that counts. If you want family members to enjoy the sound of your voice, make sure you are easy to listen to.

3. Be clear and specific. Many misunderstandings arise from muddled talk. I read about a man who, awakened out of a deep sleep when the phone rang, answered with: "You have the wrong idiot, you number!" An unclear message can only reap additional confusion. Try to think as you speak, and state clearly what you mean.

4. Be positive. In many homes 80 percent of all communication is negative. Such families become so used to faultfinding, blaming, judging, name calling, and other negative elements that such behavior becomes the norm. Be less negative and more positive.

5. Be courteous and respectful of opinions. You can do this even when you don't agree. Care as much about the other person's comfort as you care about your own.

6. Be sensitive to the needs and feelings of each family member. Develop patience and sensitivity in responding to what other family members say. If one is hurting, understand his hurt and hurt with him. If she is happy, rejoice with her.

7. Develop the art of conversation. Yes, it is an art, and the opportunities to develop it should be encouraged. Discussion on interesting subjects should be encouraged at every family gathering—mealtimes, worships, holidays, shopping trips, rides in the car, even when you're working and playing together.

The clearest examples of communication at its best come to

us in the words of Jesus as recorded in the four Gospels—Matthew, Mark, Luke, and John. In Jesus' words you will find how to reach right into the hearts and minds of others so as to heal hearts and relationships. Sit at His feet and become a masterful communicator with eternal benefits!

8. *Be willing to listen.* When listening, maintain good eye contact. Turn off the television, put down the paper, forget about cleaning the house. Focus your full attention on the other person. Act as if nothing else in the world matters except hearing the other person out. Show interest in what you are hearing by raising your eyebrows, nodding your head, and smiling or laughing when appropriate.

Ask well-phrased questions, but don't run away with the conversation. Spend less than 50 percent of the time talking. And just when you think you are through listening, *listen thirty seconds longer!*

When communication breaks down in the home, it also affects a family's relationship with God. When a family is in a state of emotional divorce, there will be a spiritual one as well. If the circuits to heaven are jammed, there will be a busy signal among family members. Someone has said that we cannot be genuinely open with God and closed to our families. Think it through!

Is Your Family a Circle or a Deadlock?

What type of relationship do you have with your family members? Very likely the pattern will resemble the leadership model established between husband and wife. In your home which of the patterns below do you follow most of the time?

1. *Authoritarian,* in which mother and/or father have complete control?

2. *Permissive,* in which the child is in almost total control?

3. *Power struggle,* in which there is intense competition among all family members for control?

4. *A cooperative relationship,* in which all members work

together for the good of the family?

Has it occurred to you that the old-style, totally *authoritarian family* has almost disintegrated? Such a family operated around fixed, rigid concepts of what constitutes ''right'' and ''wrong'' behaviors, and such concepts were not open for discussion or change. They included ideas about manners, behaviors, thinking, appearance, roles, duties, morals, and beliefs. A typical closed family opinion would be that children must always conform to what parents believe is acceptable behavior and must never argue but be punished for every deviation from rules. Such authoritarian parents usually act in good faith, for they believe that it is their *duty* to train their children and that in the end the children will benefit from such methods.

The *permissive family* style is also in big trouble, because it produces directionless living. Since there are no clear guidelines and objectives, it results in a harvest of frustrated, upset, irritable, weary, dissatisfied, and unhappy big and little people. Family members live from day to day without knowing what the next day will bring. Such families tend to break apart, with the children heading one direction and the parents another. Such a family is little more than a collection of individuals who share the same roof but who have no common goals or interests.

The *power struggle,* in which everyone is competing to win, produces intense competition. The contestants have never clarified their rules, and authority shifts from one to the other, depending on who can most cleverly outfox the other. Parents are pitted against each other and their children. Children are pitted against each other and their parents. There is no team play. It is each person for himself. Constant bickering, fighting, strife, and competition are the inevitable earmarks of this family style.

A better way exists, and many parents would utilize this better way if they only knew how. That better way—a *cooperative relationship*—begins with treating every individual in the family with respect and consideration. A person reared in such a cooperative family holds fond feelings for parents and other family members; she possesses a good measure of self-respect and is much more likely to cooperate in all family matters.

How can your family become one that enjoys one another and works cooperatively together? The best way to become a cooperative family is through a family conference in which everyone in the family has a voice in family affairs. The launching of the family conference should be a mutual decision that emerges from all family members, although it will probably originate with the parents. Children should be included in all family conference meetings, especially when the outcome of decisions will affect their lives.

What are the makings of successful family conferences?

1. *Set aside time to hold the meeting*. Family conferences must take a high priority on the weekly schedule of activities and cannot be neglected owing to overcommitments. Choose the best time of the week that fits all your needs, and make a commitment that nothing will be allowed to interfere with that time. Anticipate a time of adjustment to the new schedule. You may even miss a week or two of councils. But don't give up. Soon your family conference can become an integral part of your family routine.

2. *Select leadership*. Father or mother might be tempted to act as director or chairperson of the family conference. But the softer role you play and the more input you encourage from your children, the greater will be the rewards in the end. The heavy hand of the dictator will soon kill any progress. This does not mean you will allow a child an equal vote on all matters. It would be ridiculous to permit or foist such responsibility on an 8-year-old. But by allowing family members to have a vote in making decisions that affect them, you will build family loyalty and cohesiveness.

One idea is to rotate leadership each week, allowing each

child on occasion to be captain of the ship. It will provide excellent training for the future, encourage a rich climate for personal growth, and enhance positive attitudes toward each family member. This idea might do more to blend stepfamilies than any other single suggestion.

3. Outline chores and responsibilities. Every family situation includes a variety of necessary tasks. Frequently parents absolve their children of such responsibility because it is easier and faster to do the chores themselves. This, however, robs children of the opportunity to learn skills, to contribute their fair share to family living, and to become independent. One of the essential functions of a family council is to discuss the most effective ways of sharing responsibility and cooperating in accomplishment of tasks.

4. Provide a clearinghouse for upcoming events. The family conference offers an excellent time to announce a weekend trip, a vacation, a visit from in-laws or friends, a parent-teacher conference, or the decision to list your home for sale or construct another room. Discuss all plans and decisions that affect the family. The members will function better as a group when each has the opportunity to plan, decide, and have input regarding decisions destined to affect his or her future.

Now, this procedure of allowing a group to dialogue on a matter is much more time consuming than maintaining a dictatorship, but it is sure to increase the cooperation of group members through increased involvement. It also provides excellent training for each child's future home as well as establishing an atmosphere in which positive feelings of worth can be fostered.

It is important that you not perceive a family conference to be a new gimmick through which you can control your children; neither is it a magical way to reform behavior. These may occur as by-products of the family conference, but the purpose of the council is to improve interpersonal relationships within the family circle, to share responsibility, to communicate ideas and feelings, and to learn to enjoy one another. *The key to the effective family conference is the ability to hear what the other person is feeling—not what he is saying.*

Encourage both positive and negative feedback in your family council. Parents must be as willing to listen to their children as they wish their children to be to listen to them. The conference provides a unique opportunity for parents to hear how their children feel about their place in the family. A wise person once said that one of the best ways to persuade others is with your ears—not your mouth. Use this technique of persuasion during the family conference. God gave each of us two ears and one mouth. Do you suppose He was trying to tell us something?

The family conference is not a wonder drug that will cure all family ills. Even with an active council mistakes, misunderstandings, disputes, hurt feelings, or flashes of anger will arise. But problems are rather short-lived and quickly corrected. There is less of a repetitive pattern of the same old conflicts, as well as less rigidity, frustration, tension, repression, or retribution.

Cooperative family living provides a flexible pattern for family living that emphasizes respect, reckons with the feelings and needs of each person, and maximizes the development of personal, marital, and family potentials.

The Prime-Time Family Hour

I have noticed that often churches are dying spiritually because families are dying spiritually. Families leave the church or lose their children to the world because the family itself is falling apart. Young people are leaving many churches faster than they can be brought in. Yet the tide could be turned if families could learn the important principles necessary in conducting effective family home worships.

A conservative denomination recently polled 8,223 of its members from a cross section of North America and found that 23 percent had daily worship and another 20.3 percent usually have it. However, only 36 percent of this combined 43.3 percent were in the under-35 age category. This means that those in the child-rearing years deprive themselves and their children of the dynamics of family worship.

This same study also revealed that members who have daily family worship perceive their church and their pastor through more positive eyes, see their church more as a soul-winning church, believe it holds higher standards, and perceive its church members as more warm and friendly than do those families who neglect family worship. This group likes the pastor's sermons more and views the pastor's wife as being more effective than non-family worshipers do. Family worshipers are more active in sharing their beliefs with others, are more involved in community outreach, and have greater concern for their neighbors. They demonstrate a practical, hands-on Christianity that gives greater financial support for local outreach and that helps neighbors with their personal problems.

If daily family worship makes such a difference in the lives of Christians, what would happen to the church and the world if the daily family worshipers practiced worship morning and evening and the non-family worshipers began the practice of daily worship?

Here are some suggestions on how to put some punch into what should be the prime-time family hour in every home.

1. Schedule a convenient time that suits all family members. Scheduling can be difficult, particularly as the children get older and the family seems to scatter in all directions. To overcome a full schedule in our household, we had family worship first thing in the morning. We all got up a little earlier, and the kids all came to our bedroom and piled onto our king-sized bed. We read a short portion of Scripture and tried to make the text relevant to our lives. A couple of times each week we sat around the fireplace and read stories in the evening, had music, and planned family activities.

When the children are small, scheduling does not normally

present a lot of problems. Probably the two best times for family worship are immediately following supper or just before bedtime. Avoid attempting to sandwich family worship in between favorite TV shows or having it when the family members are tired and irritable. Give the Lord some prime time, and the key is regularity.

2. *Family worship should include music.* Small children enjoy singing songs that involve motion and action. They also like to hold things that represent what they are singing about. For instance, colored seam tape can be glued or stapled to a piece of wooden dowling. As the child sings "Who made the beautiful rainbow?" she can be waving her rainbow in the air. This gives her an opportunity to *participate* in family worship.

Let your child choose her favorite song or lead others in the singing. This gives her a part in family worship and also develops self-confidence. After a few weeks of such a program, even a very young child will be happily singing little choruses during play. How much better that is than lisping a catchy beer commercial!

3. *Plan your family worships.* Plot out a plan for worships on a calendar. Jot down ideas for stories, activities, discussions, or themes. Planned worships will take into account the developmental needs of children. Present material that shows you are in touch with each child's individual needs and developing self-identity.

Younger children love stories on almost any subject. Older children and teenagers will be interested in activities and discussions on the topics of careers, dating, sexual behavior, relationships with others, self-concept, drugs and alcohol, self-control, winning and losing, breaking bad habits, developing courage, et cetera. The fastest way to destroy family worship is to turn it into a mini-theological exegesis!

When our children were younger we tried to interject the aspect of fun and creativity into our family worships as well. Instead of solemn occasions during which family members sat stony-faced during the reading of Scripture, we encouraged creativity. Friday evening became our special family night. (In our home we observe the seventh-day Bible Sabbath, sundown to sundown, as our day of worship. When the sacred hours of the Sabbath commence on Friday evening some of our best family times begin! The seventh-day Sabbath and marriage are the two institutions that God Himself initiated in the Garden of Eden. Through the centuries He has seen fit to protect the two with His seal of approval. That's why both the Sabbath and Christian marriage are so special to us and our family. Sabbath—the happiest day of the week! Christian marriage—the ideal atmosphere in which to observe it!) We enjoyed such varied activities as guessing games, twenty questions, pantomimes, musicals, and dramas. Perhaps the most fun of all were the Bible stories acted out by the three children—Carlene directing (because she was the oldest and the bossiest), Rodney obeying willingly (because he was the most adaptable), and Mark dragging his feet (because of his nature). Their reenactments included costumes, scripts, props, and the fun of originality.

During their teen years we began a tradition of having tostadas, which we ate by candlelight on Friday evenings. Then we would sit around a crackling fire (in the wintertime) and read aloud. Sometimes we took turns reading, but together we explored many books that provided spiritual lessons and direction to our lives. Repetition cemented this practice into a family tradition, and now that our children have homes of their own, they also conduct family worship. No television, jobs, school, or extracurricular activities were allowed to invade these hours that were hallowed to God and to our family.

4. Teach without preaching. Children love stories. So worship, especially during the younger years, should include the reading or telling of character-building stories. Are there books that fill the bill? Three particular sets of books supply superior reading material for children. *The Bible Story*, a ten-volume set authored by Arthur S. Maxwell, relates the Bible stories in everyday language with artwork that makes stories come alive for young minds. Don't be surprised if these books become your children's favorites! The second set, *The Bedtime Stories*, consist of character-building stories categorized and indexed according to subject. Let's say your child has been sassy or disobedient recently. You would check the index for a story that deals with sassiness or disobedience. Without ever condemning your child's behavior, you can teach better character traits! The third set, *Tiny Tots Library*, contains three volumes entitled *Bible ABC's*, *Bible Firsts,* and *Boys and Girls of the Bible*. These books are designed for the very young child.*

5. *Talking with Jesus.* The entire family worship period should lead toward "talking with Jesus." Build toward this time with eager anticipation. Teach your child to talk to God as he would with a friend. You might try a "conversational prayer" approach. You thank Jesus for something, and ask your child to give thanks for something. Next you pray about a problem, then encourage your child to pray about a problem.

A special note to mothers. If you wish your husband to lead out in family worships, you must make it easy for him. It would be a rare man who went to the local Christian bookstore to search for songs with meaning, stories with purpose, and felt sets to illustrate a point! In most cases Mother will plan worships and purchase materials. But you can still encourage your husband to lead out. If we want the men in our lives to be the spiritual leaders of the home, we will have to help them in a subtle and meaningful manner.

Our daughter, Carlene, has done this in her home. In the family room at Brian's elbow are neat boxes containing dozens of story felts, finger puppets, and visual aids. All Brian has to do is reach for them. Carlene has developed a seminar program for

---

* If you would like more information about these colorful books, write to the publisher at Box 1119, Hagerstown, Maryland 21741.

parents of preschoolers that teaches them effective ways to weave family worship into the home. (Information about the seminar is available from the author through the publisher.)

At the time of this writing our grandson, Matthew, is 3 years old and handicapped. His vision and motor development are impaired, but this doesn't keep him from enjoying his favorite time of day. During a recent visit, when the call to worship time was given, Matthew scampered for his special "worship chair" and eagerly participated in each song and planned activity. But an interesting event occurred when worship ended: Matthew began crying! Are your home worships so exciting that your children cry when it's over? Maybe they are silently "crying" *for* worship.

A young couple, parents of three children, were experiencing what they termed "incompatibility and a lack of communication." Their troubled relationship led them to believe that the only solution was divorce—for their own sanity and for the sake of the children. Week by week Harry and I led them through the practical principles and activities outlined in our *The Compleat Marriage* book and accompanying workbook. Bit by bit they began to understand that better communication techniques can be learned and that they weren't as incompatible as they first imagined.

When we suggested that they begin having regular family worship, some real questions crossed their minds, and they began with much hesitation. Two weeks later they reported that family worship, along with private devotions, had transformed their relationship with each other and the children's behavior as well! Five years have passed, and as the family sit together in church I think what might have been if . . .

Family Togetherness—Wrapping Up the Compleat Package

The real failure of families today is the tendency to be overcommitted—not to the family, but overcommitted at work, at school, at church, with hobbies, and in the community. We tend to live life in the fast lane! A true sense of family fun and togetherness cannot develop when we live at such a breakneck speed.

In our family we promoted togetherness by cultivating certain traditions. One tradition followed for years was Mexican tostadas by candlelight every Friday evening. Even now, after all three children have left home, when they return they look forward to tostadas on Friday night. It's traditional. Birthday celebrations, holding hands during table grace, and regular family worships all became traditions through repetition. Such traditions bring a sense of belonging and closeness to a family.

This spirit of fun and creativity must have rubbed off on our children, because on the occasion of our seventeenth wedding anniversary they surprised us with an unannounced party. When Harry and I arrived home one Sunday evening, our house was packed with guests, all chosen and invited by our children. I was given a few minutes to pretty up, and then we were escorted to seats of honor placed strategically before the entire group. Carlene, the originator and director of this social event, proceeded to read in mock dignity the purpose of the evening. I hold the original in my hand:

On January the first, at eight o'clock in the evening, just seventeen short, full, happy years ago, there was a wedding at the home of Mr. and Mrs. Carl William Reel. Their daughter

Nancy Lue
was married to
Mr. Harry Arthur Van Pelt.

We would like tonight to recreate just a small part of the wonderful, wonderful evening. So-oo-oo-oo. . . . So on with the show!

Then followed a delightful evening of games, food, and music. Our children even played a recording of the wedding. The highlight of the evening occurred when the three children stood in front of us as we were again seated in the chairs of honor and presented with an envelope. With eager anticipation we opened it and read:

Dear Mr. and Mrs. Harry A. Van Pelt:

You have just received a gift trip for two, for three days and two nights, at the beautiful log cabin in Canmore, Alberta, Canada.

We hope that you will have a lovely second honeymoon and enjoy the vacation from home, children, and the regular routine. The facilities we know you know well, so rest assured that you will have no trouble, only lots of fun and a very lovely time.

All the other dates you were "supposed to have" as of now are canceled. They were all fake! A few people were involved indirectly in helping us fake you out, and they all send you all the luck in the world and the best of wishes.

The signatures of three champion children—Carlene, Rodney, and Mark Van Pelt—concluded the letter, which contained $15 they had collected among themselves for us. I don't know how this affects you right now, but my eyes are indeed misty! What precious memories of fun times we now cherish as we look back upon the days when our family was all together!

It takes time to develop a compleat family. Sort out your priorities so you understand the difference between the urgent and the important. *Slow down, Christian family, slow down*. God will bless and honor your efforts from this day forward as you follow His blueprint for happiness.

Chapter 7

The Family Beyond Tomorrow
—Is Eternity in Sight?

Man's ultimate destiny depends not on whether he can learn new lessons or make new discoveries and conquests, but on his acceptance of the lesson taught him close upon two thousand years ago.

A mid-American farm family are getting ready for their daughter's wedding; college kids are enrolling for fall classes; a girl is explaining to her father that she is going to move to the city so she can "live with" her boyfriend; a young couple are roaring down the highway on a motorcycle, crowing "Yahoo"; and an older teenager is chasing a younger sister, who is attempting to steal her contraceptive device. Ordinary people, performing ordinary activities.

In the background, cryptic TV bulletins report: "NATO armored troops are breaking through. . . . Soviet-built Mig-25s are invading West German air space.. . . . Nuclear weapons in the low-kiloton range airburst over . . ."

Suddenly American and Soviet nuclear missiles crisscross over the continents. In a blinding flash, Kansas City and its suburbs lie in rubble. Building implosions follow. Some inhabitants are vaporized, dying instantly by incineration; others die slowly from radiation poisoning. The farmland too is poisoned by radiation. Survivors rule the land by rifles.

All that is left are the devastated ruins of Kansas City in *The Day After*, a film heralded as having the "unhappiest ending in all the annals of broadcast entertainment.'' According to the November 21, 1983, issue of *Newsweek,* ''there's never been a movie like ABC's *The Day After,* nor any video event that has stirred so much ferment in so many quarters before it even arrives on the airwaves.'' And probably not on the day after, either.

But why? Because people fear that a real nuclear Armageddon is creeping ever closer. *The Day After* was terrifying, but nothing like what would happen in the event of nuclear war. Scientists from the World Health Organization have calculated that a full-scale nuclear war would kill more than 2 billion persons—nearly half the world's population—either instantly or from blast-related injuries and radiation sickness.

Through all the publicity surrounding *The Day After*, both before and after the film, I was struck with two thoughts. First, I recalled that the Gospel of Luke actually predicted such fear. ''And there shall be signs in the sun, and in the moon, and in the stars; and upon the earth distress of nations, with perplexity; the sea and the waves roaring; *men's hearts failing them for fear,* and for looking after those things which are coming on the earth: for the powers of heaven shall be shaken. And then shall they see the Son of man coming in a cloud with power and great glory'' (Luke 21:25-27).

The Day After elicited more fear than any other in movie history!

Second, I couldn't help concluding that the real issue for Christians is not ''the day after'' but rather ''the day before''! We all know we are going to pass on one way or another. But the Christian can rest secure in the hope and promise of the future. Jesus Christ promised that after perilous times He would return to earth and claim His faithful followers. Everyone in your family needs to claim the security of this promise.

Have you ever seriously considered what Earth will be like the day after Christ returns to claim His own? I have, and quite by accident. It was 10:30 A.M. on May 18, 1980. My mother, Elsie Reel, phoned from Tacoma, Washington, to my home in Fresno, California, to wish me a happy birthday. But on this particular occasion we spent far more time discussing the eruption of Mount St. Helens than my birthday! Mount St. Helens was some seventy-eight miles from her home.

Scientists and geologists had been watching the activity at Mount St. Helens since March 20, 1980, when an earthquake registering 4.1 on the Richter scale announced to the world that the giant, asleep for 123 years, was rumbling into life. Earthquakes in the area increased in frequency until by March 25 it was difficult to distinguish among individual quakes. The press called it an earthquake "storm."

Predictions of an imminent eruption ran rampant. On Thursday, March 27, one week after the first recorded earthquake, a small volcanic eruption did occur, followed by a number of other small eruptions. Soon reports came in of a tremendous traffic jam in the sky, for pilots and reporters crowded the skies. At one point radar documented more than 250 aircraft in the area at one time. A few "eager beavers" risked their lives by flying illegally into the restricted area.

Steam eruptions continued to spew from the enlarging crater. The summit of the mountain drooped while the northern flank bulged. Eruptive venting continued frequently and then almost stopped abruptly after four weeks of activity. Mount St. Helens was once again calm. During this deceptive calm, authorities took precautions to ensure public safety. The area near St. Helens and Spirit Lake, which lay directly below the danger, was evacuated. Most residents left willingly, recognizing the danger. Only 84-year-old Harry Truman, operator of St. Helen's Lodge, refused to leave. Since he had spent most of his adult life on the mountain, he had no intention of fleeing. Schoolchildren, friends, geologists, and sheriffs entreated the elderly man. The refusal of this octogenarian supported temporary confidence in the supremacy of man.

But at 8:31 A.M. on May 18, 1980, everything in the Pacific Northwest changed. When Mount St. Helens blew her top, it changed the skyline of America's Pacific Coast and the landscape of Washington State. Two magnitude 5 earthquakes rocked the area. The explosion was the equivalent of an estimated 10-megaton nuclear bomb or 10 million tons of TNT. It began with a flash of light and heat 800° to 1,000° C., spreading over a distance of twelve to fifteen miles. Everything in the direct path of the explosion itself was incinerated. The belching column shot one mile into the sky immediately, and eventually it soared to some sixty thousand feet.

Next came a roaring pressure wave that traveled at the speed of sound. Later an enormous gush of liquid rock, mixed with air and ice, comprising one and a half cubic miles of material, blasted from Mount St. Helens' angry northern face. Total devastation in a 150-square-mile area resulted.

There was no rosy dawn for most of the Pacific Northwest the next day. Instead, the ash-darkened sky rained mud, while dim red lightning flashed through the volcanic gloom. Areas of eastern Washington, northern Idaho, and western Montana had to dig out from under sixty thousand tons of gritty ash—dust that accumulated one to six inches deep on the ground. Cities had to shut down. Airports, trains, cars, and businesses of all kinds were halted by the storms of ash dust.

Mudflows jammed the once-beautiful rivers. Bridges and roads were destroyed, and countless others became impassable. Between 5 and 10 million cubic yards of mud flowed down the Cowlitz River into the Columbia River. Unknown numbers of deer, rabbits, and birds met their doom. The boiling mud destroyed 70 million salmon and trout; many of them were actually seen leaping to the shore. In addition to the ash and the destruction of property and wildlife, twenty-five persons were known dead and forty were missing.

When my mother suggested that we visit the Mount St. Helens area in 1983, I leaped at the opportunity. Starting out, we passed through the interior of Washington State and saw some of the most beautiful wooded areas in the world. Dense undergrowth, tall firs, and green foliage dressed the hillsides as far as the eye could see. We approached the St. Helens area, which also was lush and green. We detected no signs to warn us of what lay ahead. Instead, lupine and other brightly colored mountain flowers dotted the narrow logging road that took us closer to our destination.

Abruptly the greenery stopped—as if someone had cut it with a knife. The area resembled a scene from a science-fiction movie where you might discover a desolate place in which things remain standing but nothing moves. One minute we were bouncing through a heavy forest. The next, our eyes lighted upon the bleak remains of totally stripped trees. All were gray—each looking very much like its neighbor. The surrounding hills were all uniform—covered with gray ash and stark-naked trees.

As we drove closer to Mount St. Helens the terrain changed in spots. The barren trees no longer stood upright but were arranged on the ground side by side, all in the same direction—testament to the force of the blast. We stopped to view what was left of Spirit Lake. At one time a tall, symmetrical snow-capped mountain had reared up behind this beautiful, serene lake, sheltered by lush forests. Now it was only a memory. Mudflows had raised the water level two hundred feet. The Spirit Lake of today bears no resemblance to the Spirit Lake of yesteryear. Hundreds of thousands of logs jam the surface of the lake, forming an unwelcome carpet that would allow a person to walk from shore to shore.

Our last stop was Windy Ridge at the end of the road—as close as we could get to the mountain. Mount St. Helens stood with one third of her northern side nothing but a huge gaping hole. Steam still rose from inside the crater. What was left of her northern flank stretched out to the remains of Spirit Lake below. What is now called Truman Ridge lay directly across the new lake from us—where Harry Truman was immortalized beneath the lava flow. I couldn't see a living thing anywhere except the other curiosity seekers who came to explore the remains. I was awed. I was viewing the effects of "the day after"!

Several geologists had observed, mapped, collected, analyzed, then predicted the eruption two years *before* it blew; their descriptions were as accurate as any accounts to date. Therefore, if the eruption of Mount St. Helens was a surprise, it was not for lack of accurate predictions!

Yet "we relearned from this horrendous eruption that for some of nature's events, there is no warning. For many other events scheduled by nature, the warnings are there, and it is up to us to learn to read them intelligently and to help our fellowman understand their significance."—Professor Leonard Palmer, *Mount St. Helens—The Volcano Explodes*, Davenport, Iowa: Lee Enterprises Inc., 1980, p. 105.

This statement, written by a geologist, struck me with force. Even though geologists had been predicting the eruption for two years and the signs were all there, the actual event caught everyone unaware. Those within range of the blast were carrying on everyday duties, completely unconcerned of what was about to happen. Repeated predictions and warnings had been made but had gone unheeded. Governor Dixy Lee Ray had ordered everyone out of the red zone. Few paid any attention. Persons like Harry Truman and other sightseers must have assumed that they were immortal.

How frequently we act like Harry Truman regarding our own destinies. The Bible tells us repeatedly that time on this earth will come to an end, that God will stop the clock and there will be "time no longer" (Revelation 10:6). Ever since Jesus' death and resurrection, on this earth His followers have been talking about His return. Yet we live as though it will never happen. What's the matter with us? Are we truly concerned about where our family members will spend eternity?

The return of our Lord is an absolute certainty, but we do not know the day nor hour. "But of that day and that hour knoweth no man, no, not the angels which are in heaven, neither the Son, but the Father" (Mark 13:32). And what words follow this passage? "Take ye heed . . ." Perhaps you wonder how we can know that His coming is near if we don't know when it will happen. The answer is clear: by the description in the Bible of the events that will immediately precede His return. Just as the geologists predicted with accuracy that Mount St. Helens would erupt; just as we can tell when a mother is about to give birth to a child; just as we can tell when spring is about to come, so we can all know with certainty that Christ's return is "even at the doors" (Matthew 24:33).

The Bible predicts signs of His coming in the social, natural, political, and religious worlds.

The social world. The Bible declares that the period of time just before Jesus returns will be filled with a variety of dangers because it will be a self-centered, materialistic, morally bankrupt age. "This know also, that *in the last days* perilous times shall come. For men shall be lovers of their own selves, covetous, boasters, proud, blasphemers, disobedient to parents, unthankful, unholy, without natural affection, trucebreakers, false accusers, incontinent, fierce, despisers of those that are good, traitors, heady, highminded, lovers of pleasures more than lovers of God; having a form of godliness, but denying the power thereof" (2 Timothy 3:1-5).

Can you think of a more accurate description of our world today? Men and women are lovers of themselves, and therefore many are "doing their own thing." Respect for parents, school authorities, police, or anything of value or importance has almost vanished. Men and women are deserting their children and homes in an obsessive search for personal pleasure.

The race to keep up with neighbors has led to a "covetous" people in search of bigger and better things. People rob and murder for the sake of a few cents. In the name of profit, big business is allowed to pollute our world with toxic byproducts of manufacturing.

During recent years the number of people "without natural affection" has increased astronomically. Estimates indicate that a half million teenagers run away from home each year. Violence and sexual abuse in the home have taken a sharp rise. Every day multitudes of women voluntarily give up their children through adoption, abortion, or neglect. Men are deserting their wives and children as never before.

Since about 50 percent of all marriages end in divorce, "truce-breaking" is rising dramatically—in some areas it tops the charts at 70 to 80 percent! Some have likened our present family life to that of Greece and of Rome just prior to their falls. Many psychologists declare the family as we have known it is dead.

We can no longer walk the streets of our cities without fear of the "despisers of those that are good." Crime is rampant. Every newspaper, magazine, and news broadcast updates us on the latest news of a husband who plots the murder of his wife; the young person who, in a fit of rage, bludgeons someone to death; the drug-crazed teenager who strangles an elderly woman in her own home; the rapist who leaves behind him scarred victims; and the thief who must wade through blood and bodies in order to satisfy his desires. The Bible predicts that "evil men . . . shall wax worse and worse" (2 Timothy 3:13). Our prisons are overflowing, and we find no solution except the appearance of our Lord.

The natural world. Jesus predicted that an upheaval in nature would herald His coming. "There shall be famines, and pestilences, and earthquakes, in divers [various] places" (Matthew 24:7). "Upon the earth distress of nations, with perplexity; the sea and the waves roaring" (Luke 21:25).

Earthquakes, famines, and destructive storms have increased in number and velocity during recent years. Calamities by air, land, and sea abound. The eruption of Mount St. Helens was but another example.

Other bold signs in nature are graphically described in Scripture: "Immediately after the tribulation of those days shall the sun be darkened, and the moon shall not give her light, and the stars shall fall from heaven" (Matthew 24:29).

Have these prophecies come true? "On the 19th of May, 1780, an uncommon darkness took place all over New England, and extended to Canada. It continued about fourteen hours. . . . The darkness was so great that people were unable to read common print, or tell the time of day by their watches, or to dine, or transact their ordinary business without the light of candles. . . . The fowls retired to their roosts. Objects could not be distinguished but at a very little distance, and everything bore the appearance and gloom of night. The causes of these phenomena are unknown. They certainly were not the result of eclipses."—*The Guide to Knowledge, or Repertory of Facts,* edited by Robert Sears, p. 428.

About a half century later, November 13, 1833, the stars "fell," as Jesus had foretold. It remains one of the greatest meteoric displays ever registered. "From the Gulf of Mexico to Halifax, until daylight with some difficulty put an end to the display, the sky was scored in every direction with shining tracks and illuminated with majestic fireballs."—Agnes M. Clerke, *History of Astronomy in the Nineteenth Century,* p. 328.

For more than four hours people from Canada to the West Indies and from California to ships in the Atlantic Ocean breathlessly gazed at millions of meteors streaking through the sky. The light from these meteors was sufficient for people to read ordinary print with little difficulty.

Jesus foretold not only these very things but also when they would happen. These signs were to occur "immediately after the tribulation of those days" (Matthew 24:29). What days? In the preceding verses Jesus had been talking about persecution directed against His faithful followers. In Matthew 24:15 He directed His listeners to the book of Daniel and told them to understand. In Daniel 7:25 we read of a period of persecution coming upon true Christians. History reveals that this happened during the Dark Ages, when millions lost their lives for their faith. By the mid 1700s, however, the persecution had virtually ended. And amazingly, in 1780 and 1833, "immediately after the tribulation of those days," the remarkable signs foretold by Jesus appeared in the heavens!

The political world. War is the outstanding sign in the political world. "And ye shall hear of wars and rumors of wars. . . . Nation shall rise against nation, and kingdom against kingdom" (Matthew 24:6, 7).

Never before the twentieth century had war become a "world war," in which nearly every powerful nation on earth joined the fight on one side or the other. With World War II we entered the atomic age. Today we live with the knowledge that with one quick push of a button our world could become a devastated heap of smoking, lifeless rubble.

Since World War II, wars have broken out in Korea, Vietnam, Africa, the Middle East, Asia, South America, and Pakistan, to name a few countries. World leaders try to predict where the next outbreak might occur. Their greatest fear is nuclear destruction; their greatest hope is peace.

The religious world. God's Word plainly teaches that a widespread apostasy from Bible truth will characterize the last days. People will have "a form of godliness," but spiritual power will be largely missing. Paul, writing to early Christians about Jesus' return, declares: "Let no man deceive you by any means: for that day shall not come, except there come a falling away first" (2 Thessalonians 2:3).

According to many religious thinkers, the Biblical account of Creation must give way to evolution. Theologians teach that Jesus is merely human and ridicule His resurrection from the dead. "Now the Spirit speaketh expressly, that in the latter times some shall depart from the faith, giving heed to . . . doctrines of devils" (1 Timothy 4:1).

The Bible predicts that professed Christians will grow weary of hearing straight truth. "For the time will come when they will not endure sound doctrine; but after their own lusts shall they heap to themselves teachers, having itching ears; and they shall turn away their ears from the truth" (2 Timothy 4:3, 4).

Many Christian preachers teach from the pulpit that the literal second coming of Jesus will not be visible to every eye, but He will instead come individually or spiritually to each believer. Today the entire religious world has fallen into utter confusion. Those who seek truth, unless they are hardy individuals who can think and diligently study for themselves, give up rather than attempt to sort through the ever-mounting contradictions.

Jesus tells of another great event in the religious world. "And this gospel of the kingdom shall be preached in all the world for a witness unto all nations; and then shall the end come" (Matthew 24:14). This verse indicates that all the world will have an opportunity to hear about the plan of salvation before the end of time.

Despite appalling world conditions, you need not fear for the future of your family. God's plan for His earthly family is not total annihilation, but rather the glorious destiny of eternal life. Jesus, the Son of God, said, " 'Let not your heart be troubled. You are trusting God, now trust in Me. There are many homes up there where my Father lives, and I am going to prepare them for your coming. When everything is ready, then I will come and get you, so that you can always be with me where I am. If this weren't so, I would tell you plainly. And you know where I am going and how to get there' " (John 14:1-4, T.L.B.).

This promise is actually an invitation from the Lord Himself. He wants you to become part of His heavenly family. Regardless of the inadequacies of our present homelife, here we find a promise for a future that is too good to pass up! However, whatever the amount of time allotted to us on this earth, our purpose should be to resolve solemnly to create a little heaven on earth to go to heaven in. God has given us a blueprint to family happiness now and hereafter. I would like to suggest that you stop reading long enough to commit yourself to follow that blueprint for happiness. God wants to open the storehouse of heaven's blessings upon your homelife beyond your fondest expectations.

I've discovered that it's always easier to follow through on a commitment if you can have the help of a friend. You will find such a friend in the Voice of Prophecy radio broadcast's easy-to-understand home study lessons. While writing this chapter, I relied heavily upon the New Life Voice of Prophecy Bible guides. I found these free Bible lessons to be fascinating. If you have at times wondered what the future really holds for you and your family, mail the preprinted postcard inserted at the end of this chapter to the Voice of Prophecy, Box 55, Los Angeles, California 90053 and request their free New Life Bible Course. You will be under no obligation at any time. But let me assure you that enriching rewards await you.

As you purpose in your heart to please God, you will look forward with even greater anticipation to the return of Jesus Christ. It won't be long until Paul's splendid prophecy will be fulfilled before your very eyes: "For the Lord Himself shall descend from heaven with a shout, with the voice of the archangel, and with the trump of God: and the dead in Christ shall rise first: then we which are alive and remain shall be caught up together with them in the clouds, to meet the Lord in the air: and so shall we ever be with the Lord. Wherefore comfort one another with these words" (1 Thessalonians 4:16-18).

Just before it is all over here on earth, "a dense blackness, deeper than the darkness of the night," will fall upon the earth. But out of that darkness will appear a rainbow spanning the heavens, "shining with the glory from the throne of God." The black angry clouds will part, and those who love God will see "the glory of God and the Son of man seated upon His throne." And from that spot of indescribable glory, will come " the voice of God like the sound of many waters, saying: 'It is done' (Revelation 16:17)." That voice will shake the heavens and the earth.*

Soon there will appear in the east "a small black cloud, about half the size of a man's hand." It surrounds the Saviour, and in the distance it seems to be shrouded in darkness. God's people know this to be the sign of the Son of God. In solemn silence they gaze upon the cloud as it draws nearer the earth, becoming lighter and more glorious until it is a great white cloud, "its base a glory like consuming fire," and above it a rainbow. Every eye will behold the Saviour. "A diadem of glory rests on His holy brow," and "His countenance outshines the dazzling brightness of the noonday sun." And He says, "My grace is sufficient for thee" (2 Corinthians 12:9).

The King of kings will descend upon the clouds, wrapped in flaming fire. The heavens will be rolled together as a scroll, the earth will tremble before Him, and every mountain and island will be moved out of its place. Amid the reeling of the earth, the flash of lightning, and the roar of thunder, the voice of the Son of God will call forth all sleeping saints: "Awake, awake, awake, ye that sleep in the dust, and arise!" Throughout the length and breadth of the earth the dead shall hear that voice, and they that hear shall live. All will come forth from their graves the same in stature as when they entered the grave, but all blemishes and deformities are left forever behind. The last lingering traces of sin will be removed, and Christ's faithful will appear in "the beauty of the Lord our God," in mind and soul and body reflecting the perfect image of their Creator.

The living righteous will be changed "in a moment, in the twinkling of an eye" (I Corinthians 15:52). At the voice of God they were glorified; now they shall be made immortal and with the resurrected saints meet their Lord in the air. Angels will go

---

* The description of Christ's return to this earth is adapted from *The Triumph of God's Love*, by Ellen G. White, pages 555 to 570.

forth from one end of the earth to the other, gathering together the faithful and escorting them into the heavens. Little children will be carried by angels to their mother's arms. Friends long separated by death will be united, nevermore to part, and with songs of gladness they will ascend together to the city of God.

Upon the heads of the faithful, Jesus with His own right hand will place the crown of glory. Each will have a crown, bearing his own "new name" (Revelation 2:17). In every hand will be placed "the victor's palm and a shining harp." Then, as the commanding angel shall strike the note, every hand will sweep the harp strings with skillful touch.

Before the vast rejoicing throng will loom the Holy City. Jesus Himself will open wide its pearly gates. At last the faithful will enter in. There they will behold the Paradise of God—a vivid reminder of Adam's first home—the Garden of Eden. The redeemed, clothed in richer robes than the most honored of the earth have ever worn and crowned with crowns immensely more glorious than those ever placed on earthly monarchs, will stand before God's throne. The days of pain and weeping will be forever ended; every cause of grief will be removed. All will begin singing a hymn of praise clear, sweet, and harmonious; every voice will take up the melody until the anthem swells throughout all of heaven. And so shall we ever be with the Lord.

Eternal life isn't cheap, but it is free—freely given as a gift by the Lifegiver Himself. Can you think of a more glorious future for your loved ones than to possess the assurance that everyone in your family will enjoy eternal life in heaven with God? Will your circle be unbroken? Only two words will matter at that moment. What joy will fill your soul if you can only hear the Master Architect announce in tones of glowing gratitude and tenderness, "Well done." He will then invite you to "Enter thou into the joy of thy Lord" (Matthew 25:21).

You and your entire family can hear those words of divine commendation if you will abide by His blueprint for happiness—from this day forward.

Other books by Nancy Van Pelt:

- *The Compleat Marriage* and *The Compleat Marriage Workbook*
- *The Compleat Parent* and *The Compleat Parent Workbook*
- *The Compleat Courtship* and *The Compleat Courtship Workbook*
- *The Compleat Tween* (for ages 9-14)

Visit your friendly Adventist Book Center, where you'll find these books and many more to help you build better relationships and improve the quality of your life. For the name of the Adventist Book Center nearest you, call or write the publisher.

Review and Herald Publishing Association
Box 1119
Hagerstown, MD 21741
(301) 791-7000

Contact the publisher for information about seminars.

Study the Bible for yourself with
New Life Bible Guides

The Bible offers solid answers to questions like these:

- Why does God permit suffering?
- How can you get answers to your prayers?
- Will God forgive every sin?
- What is the spirit world?
- Is prophecy being fulfilled now?

Learn the answers to these questions and more. New Life Bible Guides let you study at your own pace and in your own way. And there's absolutely no cost or obligation! Fill in the coupon today and mail it to New Life Bible Guides, Box 55, Los Angeles, CA 90053.

- -

Yes! I want the answers! Send me, absolutely free, the first in your series of 34 New Life Bible Guides.

Name _____

Address _____

City _____

State _____ Zip _____